NATURE
INTO
ART

Exiguus spatio, variis sed fertilis herbis.

Engrav'd by Henry Fletcher London 1729.

NATURE
INTO
ART

A Treasury of Great Natural History Books

HANDASYDE BUCHANAN

MAYFLOWER BOOKS
NEW YORK

Library of Congress Cataloging in Publication Data
Buchanan, Handasyde.
Nature into Art.
Bibliography: p.
Includes index.
1. Zoological Illustration – History.
2. Botanical Illustration – History. 1. Title.
QL46.5.B82   500.9'02'22   79–12481
ISBN 0–8317–6337–X

Manufactured in Great Britain
First American edition

Designed by Sara Komar
House editor Esther Jagger

In accordance with standard international bibliographical practice,
where no place of publication is specifically mentioned it is always
London.
In the text and captions books with very long titles are referred to by
their commonly used short titles. More complete titles will be found in
the list on page 213.

The chapter on flowers and fruit incorporates part of an essay by the
author originally printed in *The Gardeners' Album*, edited by Miles
Hadfield, published by Hulton Press, 1954.

FRONTISPIECE The *Catalogus Plantarum*, published in London in 1730
by the Society of Gardeners, is one of the very first flower books to
contain a number of colour-printed plates. This is its frontispiece,
sometimes found coloured, but more usually uncoloured, as here.

CONTENTS

Acknowledgments

I SHOULD LIKE to express my gratitude to all those who have helped in the preparation of this book. Howard Radclyffe and the staff of Messrs Quaritch were generous with their time and assistance in providing books for photography. I am grateful to John Collins of Sotheby's for his kindness. To George Rainbird, Sir Sacheverell Sitwell and Wilfrid Blunt, with whom I was privileged to be associated in the major natural history book ventures of the 1950s, I owe a great debt of thanks; in particular to George Rainbird, who was the inspiration behind all these books and who has been especially helpful to me on this one.

For providing illustrations, or making books available for photography, I must acknowledge the co-operation of the librarians of the Linnean Society and the Royal Horticultural Society, and the staff of the Zoological and Botanical Libraries at the British Museum (Natural History). Angelo Hornak was responsible for much of the photography.

And finally I must thank Esther Jagger, without whose help this book could not have appeared, and who has done at least as much work as I have; and Geraldine Goller, who has contributed time and effort on my behalf.

Foreword

AS A CHILD I WAS very nearly completely uninterested in flowers and birds. Insects were a nuisance. Fruit and fish were good for eating. I used to collect cornelians and agates on the beach at Southwold in Suffolk. But even at five I preferred to read *Ivanhoe* or *Treasure Island* and *Kidnapped*, and at seven I had enjoyed *Macbeth*, so that 'the owl, the fatal bellman' was nearer to me than any living bird or animal. And I managed to become a bookseller at twenty-three without having improved much on this scanty knowledge and appreciation.

Somehow, thanks mostly to an elderly and wonderful assistant, I began to specialize in old books with coloured plates, all on some kind of natural history. From then onwards everything changed. Flowers meant Dr Thornton, Redouté and many, many others. Birds were Levaillant, George Edwards and so on. If I am a moderately good ornithologist it is because of old bird books. I can never be a botanist but I love flower and fruit plates. Insects for me start with Maria Sibylla Merian in 1705.

However, although I am probably, without boasting, the acknowledged expert on Dr Thornton's *The Temple of Flora*, I have never read or wanted to read Gilbert White's *Natural History of Selborne*. When left alone with a good book my choice will be something on the American Civil War, Pelham Warner's *My Cricketing Life*, or a book on railways. Or for something more literary, let it be *Macbeth* or Rostand's *Cyrano de Bergerac*. If, however, I am landed in the sale-rooms, my knowledge of any of these titles is as nothing compared with my advice – based on forty years of experience – on old natural history books with coloured plates.

Handasyde Buchanan
London
February 1979

Introduction

THE SCOPE OF THIS BOOK is the period from about 1700 to 1900 or a little earlier, and its aim is to show a selection of the best illustrations from old natural history books with coloured plates, together with an account of these books and their creators, which represent what might be called the golden age of the natural history book. It is not intended to be a complete history of books in this period, but rather a personal choice from among the best examples. The subjects cover birds, flowers, fruit, trees, gardens, animals, fish, insects and shells.

If there appears at first glance to be an imbalance in the amount of space devoted to these categories it is because the vast majority of these books were about birds and flowers, although insects are, indirectly, well represented since almost all books about them are, from the point of view of their plates, in effect flower books. Maria Sybilla Merian's *Insects of Surinam*, for instance, which first appeared in 1705, is both a flower and an insect book. Shells – because they are so pretty – receive a little more attention than perhaps they deserve. Inevitably it is animals and fish which appear least often. Fish, I suppose, needed a lot of getting hold of before they could be drawn. They lose their colours rapidly when out of water, and start smelling almost as quickly. Audubon's *The Birds of America* is one of the very greatest natural history books of all time. His other venture, *The Viviparous Quadrupeds of North America*, is a mere shadow of the birds. Explorers, collectors and artists seemed to concentrate less on animals, and when animals were drawn it was more usually for zoological reference, and such plates show a more academic and therefore less decorative and attractive approach. There are (relatively) many dull animal books, but the total output of animal books – or the proportion of general natural history books devoted to animals – was small.

At the beginning of our period – the time when books with coloured plates were first produced – the pictures were taken from copper-plate engravings, and coloured by hand. This method was used from 1700 until about 1830 when that type of illustration was outmatched by the aquatint, the mezzotint and the stipple engraving, often printed in colours. This was the finest hour of colour printing. Around 1830 the lithograph appeared, which involved printing from a stone instead of a copper plate; it was still, however, coloured by hand. But towards the end of the nineteenth century the chromolithograph, in which the colour came directly from the stone and was not applied by hand, had won the battle. Of course it made natural history books grow steadily cheaper, and was the parent of all later flower, bird and animal plates, but these illustrations lack the individual artistry that made the earlier ones fascinating and unique, and the pleasure of looking at the pictures as works of art has gone. An account of the differences between these various processes, and how each was done, appears at the end of the book, on page 193. However in the 1950s a number of superbly produced, definitive books were published, all with bibliographies and fine reproductions of plates, such as *Great Flower Books* and *Fine Bird Books*. I contributed to most of them, and this book contains five plates taken from *Fine Bird Books* to show the quality of printing that could be achieved, though expensively, by modern methods at that time. Now, only a quarter of a century later, these books have themselves become treasured, collectable items.

During the eighteenth and nineteenth centuries certain countries were at the top of what might be called the natural history book league, and this is perhaps the place to say who they were, when and why. The Dutch came first because they were the earliest explorers – Tasmania, for instance, was originally discovered by the Dutch in the seventeenth century, and known as Van Diemen's Land. Merian's *Insects of Surinam* (Surinam being a Dutch colony in northern South America at that time) of 1705 was the best example of Dutch work, although as late as 1794 a lovely and anonymous flower book called *Nederlandsch Bloemwerk* showed that the Dutch had not forgotten how to produce beautiful work. The Germans were active in the early eighteenth century, and J. W. Weinmann's *Phytanthoza Iconographia*, a mammoth book in folio format, comprising four volumes with 1,026 plates, is perhaps the most notable example. But from 1730 onwards the British really dominated the field with a very large number of great books.

There is, of course, one colossal exception in these years. France, with Redouté for flowers and Levaillant for birds, using stipple engravings expertly printed in colour, undoubtedly created the finest books of all between 1790 and 1830, despite competition from excellent works such as those of Thornton and Brookshaw in England. The United States – although of course it produced the magnificent Audubon – does not really enter into this particular discussion, since it must be remembered that Audubon's gigantic masterpiece, *The Birds of America*, was actually printed and published in London.

One interesting and sometimes confusing point is that some famous books are known by the author's name, and not by that of the artist. Redouté, the greatest of all French flower book artists, has his name on almost all the books with which he was associated –

Redouté's *Roses*, Redouté's *Liliacées*, and so on – though not always as the principal. Levaillant, however, whose name appears on most of the great French bird books of that same period, was a naturalist who travelled far, but never to my knowledge drew any of the pictures for his books – almost all were drawn by Barraband. Dr Thornton was the author of perhaps the most splendid of all English flower books, popularly known as *The Temple of Flora*, but whose real title is *New Illustration of the Sexual System of Linnaeus*. Of the justly famous plates which illustrate this book only one, the Roses, was drawn by Thornton himself. Books are sometimes known by the artist's name, and sometimes by the name of the author of whatever text they may contain. A number of different activities were involved in producing a book, and although some tasks were often performed by the same person – Benjamin Wilkes, for instance, was both author and artist of his *Butterflies* – it was quite possible for an explorer to provide the specimens, which would then be written up by someone else, illustrated by a professional artist, engraved by another hand, and perhaps hand-coloured by a whole team of people. All this explains the plethora of credits which are often to be found at the foot of natural history plates. The abbreviations used by artists, engravers and printers are given on page 197.

Although this book is only intended to cover printed books with coloured plates, it is worth saying a word or two about the original watercolours. Some artists were admirably served by their engravers and printers – despite Audubon's immense talent as a bird artist, for instance, *The Birds of America* would be less of a masterpiece were it not for the skills of Robert Havell. Other artists, however, were treated less well than they deserved, and so, perhaps unjustifiably from the artist's point of view, their books are considered less good. But all natural history artists are best judged by their original work, and anyone who has the opportunity of seeing the watercolours for *The Birds of America* at the New York Historical Society, or Ehret's *vélins* (paintings on vellum) at the Victoria and Albert Museum and the Library of the Royal Botanic Gardens, Kew, will be well rewarded for the effort.

The part played by the great Swedish naturalist Linnaeus (1707–78) cannot be underestimated. He made an enormous contribution to natural history by tabulating a completely new system of classification for plants and animals. Before Linnaeus classification had been a somewhat haphazard affair and lacked any sort of standardization. The most commonly followed system for plants had been that of Tournefort, who based his distinctions on the shape of the corolla. Linnaeus, on the other hand, defined his categories by the sexuality of plants – a system that scandalized the prurient morality of the Victorians, who felt that young girls in particular should not be exposed to such grossness! In his *Species Plantarum* of 1753, and *Genera Plantarum* (1737; fifth and most important edition, 1754), Linnaeus divided plants, after examination of their male sexual organs, into 24 classes, which in turn he subdivided into orders *vis-à-vis* their female sexual organs. The names were derived from the Greek

– lilies, for instance (as illustrated in Mrs Bury's *Hexandrian Plants*), which have six stamens, are in the class 'Hexandria' (from the Greek words for 'six' and 'male') and of the order 'Monogynia' (from the Greek for 'one' and 'female'), since they have only one style. Linnaeus was an imaginative man and did not lack a sense of humour: he described the class Polyandria (many male organs), which includes the poppy, as 'Twenty males or more in the same bed with the female'.

His new system of classification for animals was far less revolutionary than that for plants. The first edition of the *Systema Naturae*, published in Leyden in 1735, divided them roughly into quadrupeds, birds, amphibians, fish, insects and invertebrates (*Quadrupedia, Aves, Amphibia, Pisces, Insecta* and *Vermes*). In the tenth edition of 1758 he subdivided these classes, as with plants, and by this time he had recognized the importance of differentiating between mammals and other animals, thus *Quadrupedia* became *Mammalia* (and included man). But his system was not universally welcomed; Thomas Pennant, the English naturalist, wrote in his *History of Quadrupeds* of 1781 – perhaps foreshadowing the furore over Darwin's theories of evolution a century later: 'My vanity will not suffer me to rank mankind with Apes, Monkies, Maucaucos and Bats.'

While this book is concerned with the art and beauty of the natural history book rather than with its botanical or zoological merits, a number of expeditions – and subsequently books – were undoubtedly embarked on as a direct result of the availability of this relatively simple and foolproof system of classification, and lovers of old natural history books have good cause to be grateful to Linnaeus.

We have, of course, reached a stage today when no one but a fool would bet on the value of any book, because of inflation. But it is worth having a look at the past in this connection. *The Temple of Flora*, which was listed in 1890 catalogues at £20 (!), was on sale for £100 when I started as a bookseller in 1930. When I returned after the Second World War and found that the price of everything had escalated, it was then £500. By 1965 (it is now very scarce in the right state and in good condition) that price had shot up to £4,000–5,000. It may now be £12,000 or more; good copies rarely, if ever, turn up.

In 1934 I produced a catalogue (reprinted on page 199) which perhaps set a precedent. It was painstakingly produced and contained more truly well-known natural history books than any catalogue published before or since. The prices were fantastically low by any later standards, and yet very few books were sold as a result of it. I hope that those who read it now will realize that they are looking at history, and if they are old enough to have been able to collect books in 1934, what a mistake they made in not investing in those days! Ninety-eight items of flowers were offered for less than £1,200, and fifty items of birds for around £500. No. 7 in the catalogue, Duhamel du Monceau, could not be bought now for less than £10,000, and No. 3, Prévost's *Collection des Fleurs et des Fruits*, would fetch at least that sum, and possibly as much as £15,000. The whole of the original first page (the first seven items) would now come to around £25,000. An estimate for any great book must nowadays be pure guesswork, but in 1977 a very fine copy of the best edition of Redouté's *Roses* (about £500 or less in 1934) fetched £28,000 at auction.

The value of a book depends on so many different reasons – date, size (book sizes are dealt with on page 197), number of volumes and plates, intrinsic beauty, scientific merits (this is perhaps less important than it should be, and someone from a more scientific background than I should say whether this is true or not) ; but ultimately on its scarcity. There are from six to ten copies of Samuel Curtis' *The Beauties of Flora* in existence, and indeed it is likely that no more were printed. This folio volume, published between 1806 and 1820, has only ten plates. It is in effect priceless.

Not all the books described or illustrated here really merit the epithet 'great'. But they are all of the highest quality – in other words, their printed plates are among the best ever produced. The texts in these books are frequently poor, even non-existent, or merely what we would now call extended captions. Many of them were produced over a long period, as single plates, and were thus clearly meant to form picture books or to be framed – either for their decorative qualities, or for their informative value, as when describing a newly discovered animal or plant. All the plates reproduced in this book are intended to be enjoyed as things of beauty.

H.B.

FLOWERS AND FRUIT

WHEN I WAS ON HOLIDAY in France one year, there was a particular garden at which I looked daily, and in which grew a flower that I could not identify, since I am neither a botanist nor a gardener. However, I could say to myself: 'There is a coloured plate of this in Trew's *Hortus Nitidissimus.*' When I got home I went straight to the book, a huge and handsome folio published in Nuremberg in 1750, and there it was – a kind of balsam! It is an added and legitimate pleasure when looking at a garden to be reminded of Redouté by hydrangeas; of Hooker by rhododendrons; of Curtis by auriculas; and of Dr Thornton if one should chance on the American bog plant, although I have never had this final piece of good fortune.

Most old natural history books have charm; some are incredibly beautiful. It has always seemed to me – and to very many collectors too – that it is, in general, the flower books which surpass those on other subjects. But what is an old flower book? I will pass over the cave drawings and manuscripts of the ancients, and start at the invention of printing, when herbals – books which described plants and their medical uses – began to appear in increasingly large numbers; they were illustrated at first with woodcuts and later, in the seventeenth century, with copper-plate letter engravings. Some of these herbals and *Florilegia* were coloured by their contemporary owners, and it is probable that some from the later period were coloured by their publishers, since the engravings were painted before the book was bound. From then until the present day there has been an increasing spate of books with coloured plates about flowers and gardens, in some cases aimed at the botanist or gardener, in others with a more or less decorative end in view – a 'drawing-room scrap book', this kind of book would have been called in Victorian times. All of these are flower books, but an antiquarian bookseller (and probably most collectors) would make a narrower definition and would include only books published between about 1700 and 1860 with coloured illustrations – in other words, roughly the classical period which this book covers.

'Throughout the ages,' Wilfrid Blunt has written, 'the flower-painter has been tossed like a shuttlecock between the scientist on the one hand and the lover of the beautiful on the other.' It is to the latter category that this book and its illustrations are primarily addressed, though inevitably botany, and in particular new botanical discoveries, played an important part in initiating flower books.

During the early part of this period – approximately 1700–80, when the plates were made from copper engravings and hand-coloured – the best books were produced in Holland and Germany. Jan and Caspar Commelin's *Horti Medici Amstelodamensis Rariorum Plantarum* was published in two folio volumes in Amsterdam between 1697 and 1701. It has 231 plates which in some copies are hand-coloured, and are of such high quality that they were undoubtedly coloured by the artists themselves, rather than by less skilled, employed colourists. The plants depicted are from Dutch colonial possessions, and the magnificent title page is illustrated in colour on page 17. The elder Commelin, Jan, was Director of the Amsterdam Physic Gardens; when he died in 1698 his nephew Caspar completed the second volume.

Maria Sybilla Merian's *Insects of Surinam (Metamorphosis Insectorum Surinamensium, ofte Verandering der Surinaamsche Insecten)* reveals another aspect of the exotic fauna and flora discovered in Dutch possessions overseas. Although nominally an insect book, bibliophiles and booksellers have always considered it a flower book since the flowers are given at least equal importance. The first edition appeared in 1705, with 60 magnificent hand-coloured plates. The 1719 edition (entitled *Dissertatio de Generatione et Metamorphosibus Insectorum Surinamensium*) contains a frontispiece and 71 hand-coloured plates, one of which is shown in colour on page 41.

Maria Sybilla Merian's own story is an intriguing one. Although this was the beginning of the great age of botanical exploration, few artists went on expeditions; they relied on sailors and naturalists to bring them specimens. Considering the attitudes of those times, too, it took an intrepid and even eccentric woman to travel to wild, unexplored lands and draw tropical plants and insects in their native habitats. But this is exactly what she did.

Born in 1647 in Germany, of a Dutch mother and Swiss father, she was surrounded in childhood by flower artists who no doubt influenced and encouraged her. She started publishing books on European insects in 1679. In 1685 she left the man to whom she had been respectably married for many years in order to join a religious sect called the Labadists, and went to Holland to live in the sect's castle in Friesland. Probably stimulated by the sight of cabinets of gorgeous tropical butterflies brought back from Surinam (now part of Guyana), which had been deposited in the castle, she and her daughter Dorothea exchanged the security of Holland for the rigours of a sea passage to South America. Between 1701 and 1703 they made hundreds of drawings on vellum of flowers and insects, and it was there that Maria Sybilla became the first naturalist to observe the development of certain insects from egg via the stages of caterpillar and chry-

OPPOSITE A Hellebore from John Martyn's *Historia Plantarum Rariorum*, London, 1728–32, one of the earliest flower books with colour-printed engravings, most of which were from drawings by Jacob van Huysum.

Turnera frutescens, folio longiore et mucronato Miller.

Jacobo Howe de Bervico S. Leonardi
in Comitatu Hiltoniensi Baronetto

Turnera frutescens
ulmifolia Plum.

E. Kirkall fe.

salis to their final, perfect form – the 'metamorphosis' in the title of her book.

The superb result of this arduous and painstaking expedition was the *Insects of Surinam*. When Maria Sybilla was forced to return home through poor health, another daughter, Johanna, took her place and made more drawings; these were used for the second, larger edition of the book. Maria Sybilla Merian was a very remarkable woman and a brilliant flower and insect artist by any standards.

Jacob van Huysum, whose older brother Jan is internationally famous as a painter of great flowerpieces, was another very talented Dutch flower painter, who spent the last twenty years of his life in England. Most of the drawings for the plates in John Martyn's *Historia Plantarum Rariorum* (1728–32), one of the very earliest colour-printed books and the first to devote a full page to each plant, are by van Huysum. Martyn was Professor of Botany at Cambridge, and his large, impressive book was produced from a purely botanical viewpoint; its intention was to illustrate some of the exotic new Central American plants in the Chelsea Physic Garden in London. Sadly, the book was not a success. Published, as many books were at that time, in parts, it was abandoned after the first 50 plates. The colour printing is somewhat primitive compared with that of later books, but the *Historia Plantarum Rariorum* represents an important landmark in natural history books.

Robert Furber's *Twelve Months of Flowers*, published in 1730, is a totally different concept. It contains 13 folio-size hand-coloured plates from drawings by the Flemish artist Pieter Casteels; one plate forms a decorative title page, while the remaining twelve luxuriant groups of flowers in vases each represent a different month of the year. It sounds like a calendar, and was in fact a sumptuous nurseryman's catalogue, though the plants depicted for the various months do not necessarily flower at that season!

OPPOSITE Engraved frontispiece from a hand-coloured copy
of Jan and Caspar Commelin's *Horti Medici Amstelodamensis
Rariorum Plantarum*, Amsterdam, 1697–1701.

PAGE 18 April, from Robert Furber's *Twelve Months of Flowers*,
London, 1730. The copper engravings in this most glorious of nurserymen's
catalogues were made by H. Fletcher from drawings by Pieter Casteels.

PAGE 19 Title page from *The Compleat Florist*, a very enjoyable,
anonymous book attributed to J. Carwitham and J. Duke,
with hand-coloured copper engravings. It was published in London in 1747.

PAGE 20 Georg Ehret's *Plantae et Papiliones, Rariores*,
London, 1748–59, is a splendid example of the
insect-*cum*-flower book *genre*. It contains 15 hand-coloured
copper engravings of which this is Plate 9.

PAGE 21 Hand-coloured copper engraving of a Crocus
from a drawing by Ehret. Plate 35 of Vol. 1 of Trew's
Hortus Nitidissimus, Nuremberg, 1750–86.

HORTI
MEDICI
AMSTELODAMENSIS
Rariorum
PLANTARVM
HISTORIA.

Ex Typographia P. et I. BLAEV. Proſtant apud A. van SOMEREN. 1697.

1 Keysers Jewel Hyacinth.
2 Diamond d?
3 Double blossem'd Peach.
4 Single Orange Narcissus.
5 Double Endroit Tulip.
6 Glory of y.e East Auricula.
7 Double Wall flower.
7 Blush red lilly of y.e Vally.

9 British King Anemone.
10 Cælestis Anemone.
11 Amaranthus trachee.
12 Single Junquill.
13 Loves Master Auricula.
14 Double painted Lady Auricula.
15 Palurus Christs thorn.
16 White Lilly of the Vally.

17 Merveille du Monde Auricula.
18 Lady Margareta Anemone.
19 Juliana d?
20 Double Junquill.
21 Duke of Beauford Auricula.
22 Secrecy N? 1 Tulip.
23 Beau Regard Tulip.
24 Dwarf Single flowering-

25 Duke of S.t Albans
26 Turky ranuncule
   Scented.
27 Double Cuckow
28 Grand Presence.
29 Sea Pink.
30 Double flowering

APRIL

Design'd by P.t Casteels.

From the Collection of Rob.t Furber, Gardiner, at Kensington. 1730.

Ingrav'd

THE

Compleat

Florift.

Confider the LILIES of the field
— SOLOMON in all his Glory was
not array'd like one of thefe

Matth. Chap. VI, ver. 28, 29.

London:
printed for J. DUKE and Sold by
J. ROBINSON at y Golden Lyon, Ludgate
Street — 1747.

Tab. IX.

1. **CERATOCEPHALUS** *Delphinii foliis. Vaill. Act. Reg. Par.*

2. **MARTYNIA** *perennis, folie subrotundo rugose, flore coeruleo, radice dentariae. Linn.*

3. **NARCISSUS** *japonicus, rutilo flore. Corn. Canad.*

Published by G. D. Ehret, the Proprietor, June 12 1748

the true Saffron.

Londin. pinx. 1741

I. M. Seligmann excud. Norimb.

NEDERLANDSCH
BLOEMWERK.

DOOR EEN GEZELSCHAP
GELEERDEN.

Te AMSTELDAM, bij
J. B. ELWE.
MDCCXCIV.

Frontispiece

Furber produced as a sequel *Twelve Months of Fruit*, an equally glorious seedsman's catalogue. The April plate from the *Flowers* is shown in colour on page 18. One of the plants in his book was given to Furber by Mark Catesby, whose *Natural History of Carolina* (1731–43) is illustrated in the chapters on animals and birds.

Furber was a member of a small trade guild called the Society of Gardeners, which had been set up in the 1720s for the mutual protection of London nurserymen and to share new discoveries in the plant world. At their monthly meetings 'each Person of the Society brought all the several kinds of Plants, Flowers and Fruits in their various Seasons, which were there examined and compared by all the Persons present'. Shortly after its foundation the members decided to publish a four-volume series, illustrating and giving details of new plants for whose introduction they had been responsible. The work was to be called the *Catalogus Plantarum . . . A Catalogue of Trees, Shrubs, Plants and Flowers . . . Propagated . . . Near London . . . By a Society of Gardeners*. In the event only the first of the intended four volumes ever appeared, in 1730. Philip Miller, the Secretary of the Society, took charge of the project and probably wrote the text. Many of the plates are from drawings by Jacob van Huysum, and this book, which is now rare, shares with Martyn's *Historia Plantarum Rariorum* the distinction of being among the first books whose plates were actually printed in colours.

Talented and fiercely independent women seem to have flourished in the field of botanical illustration at this time. Elizabeth Blackwell's tale is as extraordinary as Maria Sybilla Merian's. Mrs Blackwell – apparently neither an artist nor a botanist – was suddenly faced with the problem of obtaining her doctor husband's release from a debtors' prison, where he was languishing after an abortive foray into the printing business. On the advice of Sir Hans Sloane, the famous London physician and patron of

---

OPPOSITE Frontispiece from Mary Lawrance's
A Collection of Roses from Nature, London, 1796–1810.
A lovely book with 90 hand-coloured etchings,
but not one for botanists!

PAGE 22 John Edwards' *A Collection of Flowers Drawn After Nature*,
London, 1783–85, is the only book whose plates were made
from soft ground etchings. This one is of Anemones.

PAGE 23 Title page, a hand-coloured copper engraving,
from the delightful but anonymous *Nederlandsch Bloemwerk*,
published in Amersterdam in 1794.

Acanthus,
Branca Urfina.

{ 1.2. Blume.
3. Frucht.
4. Samæ.

Welfche Bären-Klau.

Acanthus, Plate 89 from Vol. 1 of Elizabeth Blackwell's
A Curious Herbal, London, 1737–9. The 500 hand-coloured plates
were all drawn and engraved by Mrs Blackwell.

naturalists, who had told her that a herbal of medicinal plants was needed, the resourceful lady set herself up in lodgings near the Chelsea Physic Garden, founded by the Society of Apothecaries on a piece of land donated by Sloane, and proceeded to make drawings of the appropriate plants. The result of her initiative and labours was *A Curious Herbal, Containing Five Hundred Cuts of the Most Useful Plants Which Are Now Used in the Practice of Physick*, with 500 hand-coloured plates, which came out in 1737–9. The indirect result was Dr Alexander Blackwell's release from prison. Her efforts on his behalf certainly seem worthwhile today to anyone looking at *A Curious Herbal*, but whether they were worthwhile in other respects is debatable. A few years later, after becoming involved in some sordid political intrigue in Sweden, her husband was sentenced to death and beheaded. Mrs Blackwell's book was very successful, and an enlarged edition was published in 1757–73 by the famous Nuremberg patron, Dr Trew, who was instrumental in the career of a far more famous botanical artist, Ehret.

In the early eighteenth century Johann Weinmann was a well-known pharmacist in Regensburg in southern Germany. His monumental *Phytanthoza Iconographia* (1737–45) contains 1,206 plates in four folio volumes. Among the artists he employed was Georg Dionysius Ehret, a giant among flower painters and the most important influence on eighteenth-century botanical painting.

Ehret was born in 1708, of a poor Heidelberg market gardening family. As a boy he was apprenticed to a gardener, and eventually was put in charge of a garden belonging to the Elector of Heidelberg, where he was noticed by the Margrave of Baden who offered him employment. Ehret had received drawing lessons when he was a child, and now he spent much of his free time drawing and painting the flowers in the Margrave's garden. Forced into resigning his position through the envy of his colleagues who felt he was being given preferential treatment, Ehret first travelled south-east to Austria, and then returned to Germany where he met Weinmann in Regensburg. Weinmann was a bad employer and patron, paid Ehret very little for his drawings for the *Phytanthoza Iconographia*, and even tried to wriggle out of some of his financial obligations. Ehret's talents were recognized some time later by a far more worthy patron, Christoph Jakob Trew, a Nuremberg doctor. Trew commissioned from Ehret quantities of large-sized flower paintings, and eventually Ehret was able to leave Weinmann's unsatisfactory employment and travel through Europe, drawing plants for his new patron and sending him the results. In due course, via France and Switzerland, Ehret found his way to England, where he met Sir Hans Sloane and Philip Miller, whose sister-in-law, Susannah Kennet, Ehret subsequently married.

From England Ehret journeyed to Holland, where he met Linnaeus. He readily understood Linnaeus' new system of differentiating plants, and drew a descriptive plate for it. Poor Ehret! At the time he wrote: 'Linnaeus and I were the best of friends . . . .' Later Linnaeus reproduced Ehret's Tabella, but without giving him credit for it, in the *Genera Plantarum*. Ehret returned to England in 1736, where he enjoyed the

Aloe tuberosa seu yucca gloriosa major.

patronage of Sir Hans Sloane and the Duchess of Portland, among others; he remained in England until his death in 1770, having in the meantime been made a Fellow of the Royal Society. Some of his superb work is illustrated in colour on pages 20 and 21, with plates from Trew's *Hortus Nitidissimus*, which appeared in three volumes in Nuremberg between 1750 and 1786, and from his own *Plantae et Papiliones Rariores*, published between 1748 and 1759.

The anonymous *The Compleat Florist* of 1747, usually attributed to Carwitham and Duke, is not in the same class as Ehret's work but is nevertheless very enjoyable and typical of English flower books of a practical nature at this time. Its very pretty title page is shown in colour on page 19. Philip Miller's *The Gardener's Dictionary* went slightly better in that some of the plates were by Ehret. The *Dictionary*, compiled by Miller with the help of various other contributors, first appeared as a small folio edition in 1731 and was the forerunner of hundreds of later gardening dictionaries. It had many different editions; the illustration in this book is the frontispiece from the 1755–60 one, which had 300 plates.

John Hill, author of *The British Herbal: An History of Plants and Trees Natives of Britain*, is another of the slightly eccentric figures who seem to crop up regularly in the history of old flower books. His year of birth is uncertain; as a boy he was apprenticed to an apothecary, but later he drifted into a number of diverse fields, including gardening, writing and in particular the theatre. *The British Herbal* came out in 1756. In 1759, and for the next sixteen years, he was occupied in bringing out a monumental, 26-volume work called *The Vegetable System*. Sadly, as with many undertakings of this magnitude, the money ran out, and Hill turned his hand to quack medicine. He was a prolific author and produced some seventy or eighty books, by no means all in the field of natural history.

A considerable achievement in Italy at this time was Giorgio Bonelli's *Hortus Romanus* (1772–93). Among the artists of its 800 plates was a talented lady called Magdalena Bouchard. The book is now rare. From Vienna came the vast opus of Nicolaus Joseph von Jacquin. Von Jacquin, born in 1727, was a Dutchman from Leiden who sought a career in Vienna. The Dutch, famous throughout Europe for their creativity and skill as gardeners, had been employed since 1753 on laying out the gardens at Schönbrunn Palace. Von Jacquin, then a student in Vienna, became associated with the gardens and soon, through the patronage of the Emperor, was appointed Director. Under his aegis the Schönbrunn gardens became famous, especially for the marvellous and rare tropical plants that flourished there, many of them from Dutch colonial possessions and in particular southern Africa. Von Jacquin and his gardeners themselves went on a number of collecting expeditions to distant parts and, since he also drew all 264 plates for his first great book, the *Selectarum Stirpium Americanarum Historia* of 1763, this makes von Jacquin one of the all-rounders of old flower books.

The Florist (The Florist, Containing Sixty Plates of the Most Beautiful Flowers Regularly

OPPOSITE *Aloë tuberosa*, a hand-coloured engraving from
Weinmann's *Phytanthoza Iconographia*, Regensburg, 1737–45.
Many of the drawings for the plates
were the work of Georg Dionysius Ehret.

Engraved frontispiece to Philip Miller's *The Gardener's Dictionary*, London, 1731. This plate is from the enlarged 1755–60 edition, which contained plates from drawings by Ehret, among others.

Hand-coloured engraved frontispiece to John Hill's
The British Herbal, London, 1758. It is inscribed:
'The Genius of Health recieving [*sic*] the tributes of Europe, Asia,
Africa and America, and delivering them, to the British Reader.'

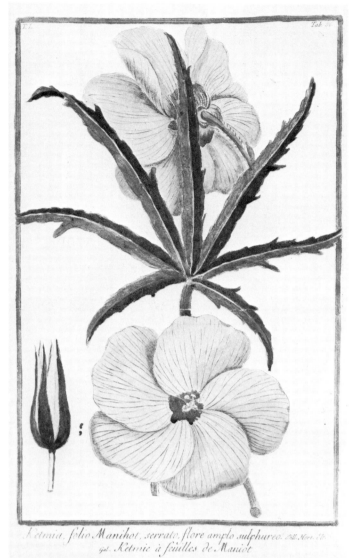

Disposed in Their Succession of Blowing . . .), by Robert Sayers and others, is an attractive though not particularly important book. It was first published in a small quarto about 1760. As with a number of flower books, the plates were not produced in a coloured version but were intended to be coloured by the purchaser – a kind of colouring book for adults – and *The Florist* contained instructions to this end. Carington Bowles reissued it in 1774–7, with re-engraved plates, including several new ones, as *Bowles's Florist*.

John Edwards' *A Collection of Flowrs Drawn After Nature and Disposed in an Ornamental and Picturesque Manner*, folio, 1783–95, is quite unique in the manner of its production. The 79 plates were reproduced from soft ground etchings; Edwards used 'light' only for the etched tints, and it is possible to think that one is looking at a pure watercolour. Wilfrid Blunt calls the plates 'decorative but stylized', but to me it is one of the greatest of all flower books. Edwards' Anemones are shown in colour on page 22.

ABOVE Ketmia, Plate 56, a hand-coloured engraving from Vol. 1
of Giorgio Bonelli's *Hortus Romanus*, Rome, 1772–93.

Plate 172, a hand-coloured engraving by F. Scheidl from Nicolaus
von Jacquin's *Hortus Botanicus Vindobonensis*, Vienna, 1770–6.

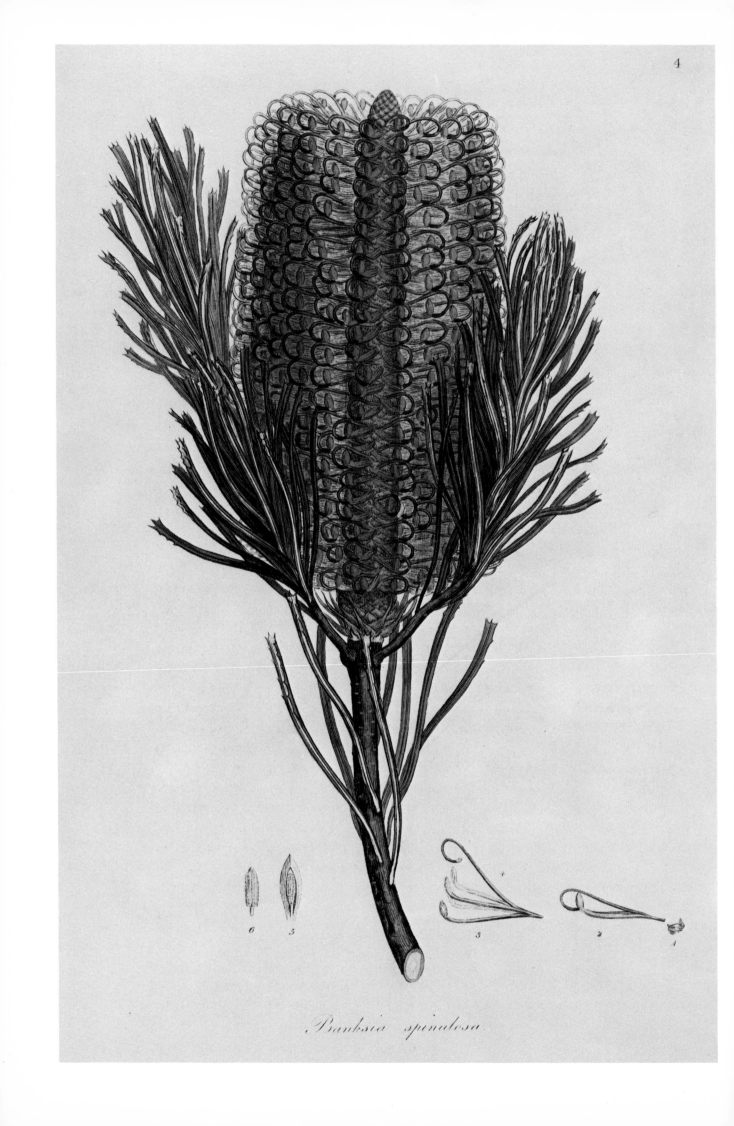

Banksia spinulosa.

George Shaw's *Zoology and Botany of New Holland* of 1793 is important for two reasons. First, it is one of the very earliest books to describe and illustrate the flora and fauna of Australasia. Second, its 12 plates were drawn by the justly famous James Sowerby, whose name is associated with a number of other great books of this period. Born in 1757, Sowerby came from a background of artists and was to start a family tradition of natural history illustration that continued for several generations. After the usual art training, in 1787 he started making drawings for Curtis' *Botanical Magazine*, which was founded in that year by William Curtis as a kind of beautifully illustrated but practical manual for growing exotic garden plants. Sowerby's *magnum opus* was his *English Botany*, a vast undertaking which came out between 1790 and 1814 and contained 2,592 hand-coloured engravings. The author of the text was Sir James Edward Smith, who – unusually – realized the over-riding importance of Sowerby's plates and did not let his own name appear even on the title page. Sowerby also engraved the majority of the plates in another great work, Sibthorp's *Flora Graeca*, which will be discussed later.

The Netherlands produced some of the best books in the early eighteenth century, and right at the end of the century, in 1794, there appeared in Amsterdam another lovely work – the anonymous *Nederlandsch Bloemwerk*, the title page of which is illustrated in colour on page 23. The turn of the century marked the beginning of the great period of English books, and at about the same time as the *Nederlandsch Bloemwerk* Mary Lawrance's *A Collection of Roses from Nature* (1796–1810) began to appear. Others who are perhaps more interested in the botanical importance of flower books regard this as a pretty book, and nothing more; but to me it is superb. Its hand-coloured frontispiece is shown in colour on page 24.

The Bauer brothers were another family 'team' who produced some of the very finest work in the history of flower illustration. Franz and Ferdinand Bauer were of Viennese origin, born in 1758 and 1760 respectively. Ferdinand first enters the scene when John Sibthorp, passing through Vienna, discovered him and took him as an artist-companion on his travels in the Balkans, which were eventually to result in the *Flora Graeca*. At his brother's instigation Franz came to England, where he met Sir Joseph Banks who, recognizing Franz's artistic talents, made him a kind of artist-in-residence at the Royal Botanic Gardens at Kew. Banks himself was one of those gifted and generous men of science, like Sir Hans Sloane, who used their wealth and influence to offer encouragement and patronage to young, struggling scientists and artists.

Franz, who did not share his brother Ferdinand's adventurous spirit, remained at Kew until he died in 1840. He was able to draw thousands of new plants brought there by those who were opening up the hitherto unknown regions of the world. Some of these drawings were published as the 30 excellent plates in *Delineations of Exotick Plants Cultivated in the Royal Gardens at Kew* (1796–1803). During his time at Kew he also gave drawing lessons to Queen Charlotte, who had some talent, and to Princess Elizabeth, who did not.

OPPOSITE *Banksia spinulosa*, Plate 4 of George Shaw and
James Smith's *Zoology and Botany of New Holland*, London, 1793.
All the plates were drawn and engraved by James Sowerby.
The book is important both for its rarity and because it is
among the very first works to contain plates of Australian plants.

With the dawn of the nineteenth century we come to two giants – Thornton and Redouté. Thornton, born sometime in the 1760s, was destined for the church but chose instead to study medicine at Cambridge. As a child he had been passionately interested in natural history; a magazine article published in 1803 contained the information that 'his grandmother often used to say, that she disliked young Thornton, as he was always catching of insects and butterflies in her garden, instead of minding his books.' His father had died when Thornton was in his infancy; after the deaths of his mother and elder brother the newly qualified doctor inherited the family money, and the idea of producing *The Temple of Flora* began to germinate in his mind.

In 1807 Dr Thornton produced his book – whose other, more official title is *New Illustration of the Sexual System of Linnaeus* ('New' to avoid confusion with John Miller's book, published in 1777, *An Illustration of the Sexual System of Linnaeus*) – in honour of the great Swedish botanist. He employed the best artists and engravers, including

ABOVE Plate 67, a hand-coloured engraving from a drawing
by Franz Andreas Bauer in his *Delineations of Exotick Plants Cultivated
in the Royal Gardens at Kew*, London, 1796–1803.

CONTENTS

I

ÆSCULAPIUS, FLORA, CERES and CUPID,
Honouring the
Bust of Linnæus

II
Cupid inspiring Plants with Love

III
Sexual System of Linnæus.

Bartolozzi, that he could find. The result was plates of unsurpassed richness, a magnificent piece of Romantic art. Thornton's pictures are from aquatint, mezzotint or stipple engravings, partially printed in colours and finished by hand. Plate 14, The Night-Blowing Cereus, is illustrated in colour on page 43. An atlas folio, and greatest of all English flower books, it was nevertheless a commercial failure and had to be stopped when half completed because of lack of support. The usual way of producing an expensive book such as this was to publish it in parts, having advertised and canvassed it in advance, and this was how *The Temple of Flora* originally appeared between 1799 and 1807. The pictures are almost unique in that the flowers are all drawn against a Romantic landscape background.

Only one of the plates, the Roses, is by Thornton's own hand. Thornton stated that he 'directed' the plates, and it would be unfair on him to underestimate the importance of this rather vague phrase. The idea was all Thornton's, as was – unfortunately – his

ABOVE The title page of Thornton's *The Temple of Flora*,
London, 1807; 31 plates are listed, although the actual
number varies from copy to copy.

choice of poetry to accompany the plates. His own prose style was aptly described by Sacheverell Sitwell as a 'mixture of royal and tropical flavour that could as well be describing the chandeliers in the Brighton Pavilion'.

Thornton lost money heavily on the venture and in 1811 obtained Parliament's permission to conduct a lottery, for which individual prints and copies of the book, in which the plates are much worn and a pale shadow of the earlier ones, were given as prizes. The lottery, too, was not a financial success since Thornton advertised a prize for each two tickets, price two guineas each! But all this means that from a collector's point of view it is the most fascinating flower book ever published. The three frontispieces present no problems, but of the remaining 28 plates listed, six more replaced six of the original plates. Some appeared in the original edition, while some were done for the 1810 edition (published in 1811, but the title page says 1810). The real difficulty is the number of states of the plates, since very few had only one state (usually the earlier state is better); some plates had at least three. Those 34 plates had 63 different states. In addition, every time a fresh print was pulled off the plate it was slightly different from its predecessor. Therefore *The Temple of Flora* is the most difficult of all books to sum up.

Only two books can justifiably be compared with Thornton's *The Temple of Flora*. The first is Samuel Curtis' *The Beauties of Flora*, one of the rarest of all flower books, with just 10 plates by Clara Maria Pope which, like Thornton's, are very unusual in that all but two of the groups of flowers are depicted against landscape backgrounds. One of these plates is illustrated in colour on page 65. The other is George Brookshaw's *Pomona Britannica* of 1804–12, containing 90 aquatint plates of all kinds of luscious-looking fruit. (The numbering is strange, running from 1 to 93 – three of the intended plates never appeared.) Like Thornton, the book is on a giant scale, but unlike Thornton all the backgrounds are plain black, brown or white. This does not, however, detract from the dramatic effect, since many of the fruit are tropical and brightly coloured, so the plain, dark backgrounds show them off to best advantage. Two of the plates are shown in colour on pages 42 and 46. Thornton only has 31 plates compared with Brookshaw's 90, but Thornton's use of greater artists, his combination of mezzotint and aquatint, and the wonderful scenic backgrounds really do make *The Temple of Flora* the better book. Brookshaw, a drawing master, described his book as 'a collection of the most esteemed fruits at present cultivated in this country together with the blossoms and leaves of such as are necessary to distinguish the various sorts from each other'. Many of his fruits were drawn in the gardens at Hampton Court Palace.

The greatest of all flower artists for the brilliance of his talent, the prolificity and consistency of his output, and not least his astonishing ability to survive and flourish under three different political regimes, must be Pierre-Joseph Redouté. Born in 1759, this highly sensitive but physically repulsive man, who was described by one nineteenth-century writer as 'a stocky figure with elephantine limbs; a head like a flat Dutch cheese . . .', was the greatest flower painter of his day, and to me the greatest of all time.

His birthplace was in a part of northern Europe that has alternated throughout history between Belgium and Luxembourg, though it was in France that he achieved his fame. As a young man he worked as an itinerant artist, and in 1782 he went to seek his fortune as a flower painter in Paris, where his brother had already gone. Redouté soon acquired a botanically orientated patron, L'Héritier de Brutelle, for whom he began the series of pictures that became the plates for de Candolle's *Histoire Naturelle des Plantes Grasses* – a natural history of succulents – which began to appear in 1798. Just before the Revolution Redouté was offered a court appointment which involved giving drawing and painting lessons to the ill-fated queen, Marie Antoinette. Although she had neither interest nor talent, she loved flowers, and while she was in prison Redouté was summoned to paint for her a cactus that was said to bloom only at midnight. This was the first royal patronage that Redouté received, though by no means the last.

Apart from the influence of L'Héritier de Brutelle, and probably also that of Jan van Huysum, whose work he had seen and admired in Amsterdam, Redouté's chief mentor was his teacher, the Dutch artist Gerrit van Spaëndonck. Van Spaëndonck's only work to be published in his lifetime was his *Fleurs Dessinées d'après Nature*, which came out in Paris in 1801. Its 24 plates are from very fine stipple engravings. He originated the technique of using watercolour alone, rather than the heavier medium of gouache, in his flower paintings, and Redouté carried on the tradition of his master. Van Spaëndonck encouraged both Pierre-Joseph and his brother Henri-Joseph, another flower painter, who was to accompany Napoleon's expedition to Egypt in the capacity of scientific draughtsman.

After the Revolution Redouté received further patronage in the person of the Empress Josephine, and it was under her aegis that he executed the paintings for two books on the gardens at Malmaison, books which are more commonly known by their authors' names than by that of Redouté. Josephine's passion was for filling the gardens of her palace at Malmaison with rare and exotic plants to remind her of her Creole background in the West Indies – plants that are depicted in all their glory in Ventenat's *Jardin de la Malmaison* of 1803–5 and Bonpland's *Description des Plantes Rares Cultivées à Malmaison et à Navarre*, of 1813–17. Of the Bonpland book's 64 plates 54 are by Redouté, nine by another extremely talented artist called Pancrace Bessa, and one is anonymous. All 124 plates in Ventenat are by Redouté.

Redouté was responsible for, or contributed to, over fifty books. Every one of his drawings was perfect, and was perfectly reproduced – and *Les Liliacées* has 486 plates; *Les Roses* 168; *Choix des Plus Belles Fleurs* 144. Plates from *Les Liliacées* and the *Choix des Plus Belles Fleurs* are illustrated in colour on pages 47 and 48.

After van Spaëndonck's death in 1822 Redouté assumed his role of fashionable drawing master to the wealthy and aristocratic. The daughters of the Duc d'Orléans – later to become King Louis-Philippe – were among his pupils, and he became sufficiently respected to be awarded the Légion d'Honneur. In spite of his idolization by the rich and influential in French society Redouté was at heart a humble man. In his time at Malmaison he had one day met Napoleon walking in the gardens. When the Emperor asked him why he had chosen to restrict himself to such a narrow field as flower painting, Redouté is said to have replied: 'I never had sufficient education to be a painter of history. Therefore . . . I wanted to be a master in a less elevated sphere . . . .' Redouté's later years were dogged by lack of money – his own fault, for he had always been a lavish spender. He died in 1840 of a stroke, while examining a white lily brought by one of his pupils, and his death was to mark the end of the golden era of French flower painting.

Palisot de Beauvois' *Plantes d'Oware et de Bénin, en Afrique*, published in Paris between 1805 and 1821, is very much in the Redouté tradition of flower painting. It contains 120 fine coloured plates of tropical flora from French possessions in West Africa. An extremely rare book, only about 20 copies were ever produced. A contemporary book from England, Henry Andrews' *Geraniums, or a Monograph of the Genus Geranium*, which appeared in 1805, is interesting for containing many species from the south of Africa. Little is known about Andrews, who produced a number of other books, notably on heaths, and drew illustrations for a periodical called the *Botanists' Repository*, a rival of the better-known *Botanical Magazine*.

Following even more in the great French tradition is the work of Jean Louis Prévost; two of the plates from his *Collection des Fleurs et des Fruits Peints d'après Nature* of 1805 are illustrated in colour on pages 44 and 45. This book, with its 48 lovely plates of flowers and fruit, is not as beautifully painted as are the works of Redouté, but it has a tremendous attraction and in a way I would rather possess it than any of the books made famous by Redouté. It is also incredibly rare. The arrangement of the flowers

OPPOSITE Maria Sybilla Merian's *Insects of Surinam*,
produced in Amsterdam in 1705, is, in spite of its title,
one of the finest of all flower books. This hand-coloured
copper engraving is from the 1719 edition, which was augmented
by plates from drawings by the artist's daughter, Johanna.

PAGE 42 George Brookshaw's *Pomona Britannica*, London, 1804–12,
is perhaps the most sumptuous of all books on fruit. It contains
90 aquatint plates, of which this is Plate 44, the Smooth-Leaved Antigua Pine.

PAGE 43 The Night-Blowing Cereus, from Thornton's
The Temple of Flora, London, 1799–1807. A number of artists
collaborated on the paintings for the plates in this
masterpiece of Romantic art, which were produced by
various techniques: aquatint, mezzotint and stipple engravings.
This one is inscribed: 'The Flower by Reinagle, Moon-light
by Pether'. Thornton himself 'directed' the plates.

PAGES 44 AND 45 Two colour-printed plates from
Jean Louis Prévost's *Collection des Fleurs et des Fruits Peints d'après Nature*,
Paris, 1805. On the left is Plate 9, showing *Tulipa Gesneriana*,
with Double Paeonies and Apple Blossom. Plate 42, on the right,
is of Double Poppies with a variety of tiny insects.

P. Sluyter Sculp.

by Reinagle. Moon-light by Pether.   Dunkarton sculp.

The Night Blowing Cereus.

London Published May 20 1800, by D. Thornton.

A Paris, chez Vilquin, M.ᵈ d'Estampes, grande cour du Palais du Tribunat. N.º 48.

Pl. 42

PLATE LXX
London Published as the Act directs by the Author & Hereshaw 1803

Iris Monnieri.   *Iris de Lemonnier.*

and fruit into pleasing bouquets and groups was intended to assist fabric designers and china painters; it is really a book of patterns, and a very superior one too.

So much for the great age of the flower book in France. Some admire Prévost's work best, while others, including me, think that Redouté was the greatest master of them all. There are other artists, too – such as Pierre Jean François Turpin, Pierre-Antoine Poiteau and Madame Vincent, who cannot all be represented here since it would be impossible to include every artist worthy of illustration. Turpin and Poiteau collaborated in making drawings for Duhamel du Monceau's *Traité des Arbres Fruitiers*, a very fine book on fruit. Of one thing, however, there can be no doubt: that France at this time reigned supreme.

The Austrian-born Ferdinand Bauer, brother of Franz Bauer of Kew Gardens fame, was responsible for the 966 plates in one of the most important and beautiful of English books at this time: Sibthorp's monumental *Flora Graeca*, whose 10 volumes appeared at various times between 1806 and 1840. Sibthorp, an Oxford professor, met Bauer in 1796 while he was passing through Vienna on his way to the Balkans, and took the young artist along to draw the plants which were the purpose of his journey. They travelled via Crete and the Greek islands to Turkey, then visited Cyprus and what is now Yugoslavia. Sibthorp undertook a second Balkan journey in 1794–5, this time without Bauer who was preparing from his rough sketches finished drawings for the projected *Flora Graeca*. Sibthorp returned in poor health, and died soon after.

The *Flora Graeca*, massive in conception, started to come out under the auspices of J.E. Smith in 1804, and was eventually finished, many years later, by J. Lindley. Its superb quality extends also to the printing of the text. One of the magnificent title pages is shown in colour on page 66. Of the original issue only 25 sets were published, so that

OPPOSITE *Iris Monnieri*, a colour-printed plate from
Vol. IV of Redouté's *Les Liliacées*, Paris, 1802–16,
one of the greatest of all flower books.

PAGE 46 A Melon from Brookshaw's *Pomona Britannica*.
Although this book does not have the same dramatic
backgrounds as *The Temple of Flora*, the aquatint
plates are still very imposing.

PAGE 47 *Tulipe de Gesner*, a colour-printed and hand-finished
plate from Redouté's *Choix des Plus Belles Fleurs*,
Paris, 1827–33. This work is not one of Redouté's best books,
but in some ways it is the most enjoyable.

ALOE rhodacantha. ALOES à épines rouges.

very few booksellers or bibliophiles have had a copy pass through their hands. 'Flaxman designed [Sibthorp's] tomb,' wrote Wilfrid Blunt, 'but the *Flora Graeca* remains his true monument.'

Thomas Knight's *Pomona Herefordiensis: Containing Coloured Engravings of the Old Cider and Perry Fruits of Herefordshire*, of 1811, is a very different book altogether. Unlike Sibthorp or Redouté it warrants no superlatives, but it is a very genial book; one of its very pretty plates – the Orange Pippin – is illustrated in colour on page 68. Giorgio Gallesio's *Pomona Italiana*, published in Pisa between 1817 and 1839, is a rather grander fruit book. It has about 170 very fine colour-printed plates (the number varies from one copy to the next). Italian booksellers in particular have never had any doubts about Gallesio's merits. A contemporary French fruit book, the *Histoire Naturelle des Orangers* of J. Antoine Risso, 1818–20, benefits considerably from having 109 colour-printed plates by the gifted fruit painter Poiteau.

ABOVE PLATE 14, *Aloë rhodacantha*, a colour-printed engraving
from a drawing by Redouté in de Candolle's
Histoire Naturelle des Plantes Grasses, Paris, 1798–1829.

Hibiscus Heterophyllus

Samuel Curtis' *The Beauties of Flora* of 1806–20, one of Thornton's rivals, had plates in the grand, dramatic manner by Clara Maria Pope, as did his *A Monograph of the Genus Camellia* of 1819. Mrs Pope was one of a long line of 'lady artists' of varying talents in the history of flower painting. Although *A Monograph of the Genus Camellia* has only five plates, they are so good that they make it one of the greatest of all flower books. It also contains very reliable instructions for cultivating camellias.

Of books from the New World at this time, two interesting examples are William Barton's *A Flora of North America*, which appeared in three volumes in Philadelphia during 1821–3, and Michel Etienne Descourtilz' *Flore Pittoresque et Médicale des Antilles*. The Barton book is one of the earliest of natural history books produced in America, and is extremely rare. Descourtilz' book has 600 plates, colour-printed and finished by hand, by Jean Théodore Descourtilz, famous as a tropical bird artist.

Two very good books with illustrations of some of the more showy exotic plants

ABOVE *Hibiscus heterophyllus*, a colour-printed, hand-finished
stipple engraving from a drawing by Redouté, from
Ventenat's *Jardin de la Malmaison*, Paris, 1803–5.

Lavatera, a plate from van Spaëndonck's *Fleurs Dessinées
d'après Nature*, Paris, 1801. The engravings were partly
colour-printed and finished by hand.

Plate 127, *Rosa turbinata*, colour-printed and hand-finished,
from Redouté's *Les Roses*, Paris, 1817–24.

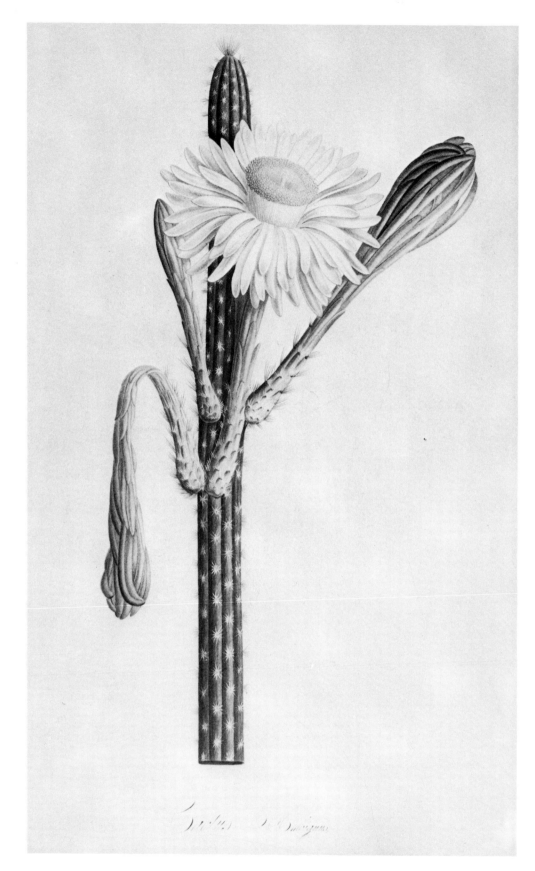

Cactus ambiguus, from Bonpland's *Descriptions des Plantes Rares Cultivées à Malmaison et à Navarre*, Paris, 1813–17. Most of the coloured plates, including this one, were from drawings by Redouté. The remainder were by Pancrace Bessa.

Pl XLII

VENTENATIA GLAUCA

Ventenatia glauca, a coloured engraving from
Palisot de Beauvois' *Plantes d'Oware et de Bénin,
en Afrique*, Paris, 1805–21.

Pesca carota, a colour-printed plate from
Giorgio Gallesio's *Pomona Italiana*, Pisa, 1817–39.

BERGAMOTTE MELLAROSE A FLEUR DOUBLE.

Bergamotta mellarosa a fiore doppio.

Poiteau pinx.ᵗ   Tab. 56.

Plate 56 of Risso and Poiteau's *Histoire Naturelle
des Orangers*, Paris, 1818–20. The colour-printed plates
were all from drawings by Poiteau.

Sasanqua Camellia

Single White Camellia   Single Red Camellia

appeared round about this time in Liverpool, at first glance an unpromising source of fine books on flowers, since it did not have a reputation for botanical artists or printers and engravers. But at this time it was the second city in England, having extensive trading connections with the Southern States of America, and the influence of William Roscoe, a wealthy local businessman with a keen interest in books and botany, was undoubtedly the catalyst. Plates from Roscoe's *Monandrian Plants* of 1826–9 and Mrs Edward Bury's *Hexandrian Plants* of 1831–4 are shown in colour on pages 71 and 69. Liverpool was, as the book titles suggest, a stronghold of the Linnaean system of classification, which was at that time not as universally accepted as it had once been. Roscoe's book was both produced and published in Liverpool, but Mrs Bury, a Liverpool lady and amateur artist, had hers engraved and printed in London by Robert Havell – to achieve greater fame as Audubon's indispensable collaborator on *The Birds of America*. Roscoe's book has 112 hand-coloured lithographs by a number of artists, including his daughter-in-law, while Mrs Bury's contains 51 aquatint plates, partly printed in colour and partly hand-coloured, which are greatly enhanced by the presence among the flowers of decorative butterflies (though frequently plants and butterflies are quite arbitrarily juxtaposed, without reference to their country of origin!).

Another English book on exotic plants – but one that really deserves to stand on its own, for it is unique in all ways – is James Bateman's colossal *The Orchidaceae of Mexico and Guatemala* of 1837–43. Wilfrid Blunt calls it 'the largest, the heaviest but also probably the finest orchid book ever issued'. It is certainly one of the best flower books with lithographic plates – 40 of them, one of which is illustrated in colour on page 70. The lithographs were executed by M. Gauci, who was a master of his craft and achieved the subtlest of gradations. Bateman himself had a sense of humour and commissioned a number of typically miniscule engravings from George Cruikshank to contrast with the enormity of the rest of the book.

The French tradition had not totally expired with the death of Redouté. The 300 plates in Lorenzo Berlèse's *Iconographie du Genre Caméllia*, Plate 35 of which is shown in colour on page 72, were drawn by J. J. Jung, and the whole book is a very considerable achievement. It came out in three volumes in Paris between 1839 and 1843.

The Victorian age – and with it, sadly, the demise of the flower book – can truly be said to have begun with the four books in what might be called Mrs Loudon's 'Ladies' Flower Garden' series. *The Ladies' Flower Garden of Ornamental Bulbous Plants*, illustrated here, is certainly not an important book, but it is very pleasant and the plates are most attractive. It was aimed at a popular audience and contained 58 hand-coloured lithographs from drawings by the author. Mrs Loudon's books, first produced in the 1840s, were reissued a decade or so later with far poorer-quality plates – a symptom of the beginning of the end of good flower books.

Sir Joseph Dalton Hooker was the son of the great botanist Sir William Hooker

OPPOSITE Single White and Single Red Camellias, one of the
five magnificent aquatint plates from drawings by
Clara Maria Pope in Samuel Curtis' *A Monograph
of the Genus Camellia*, London, 1819.

Plate 41, a hand-coloured plate of *Tradescantia Virginica* from
an early American-produced natural history book,
William Barton's *A Flora of North America*, Philadelphia, 1821–3.

Pl. 62

Théodore Descourtilz Pinx.

Gabriel Sculp.

GRENADILLE SANS FRANGES.

Plate 62, a colour-printed, hand-finished plate from a drawing
by Jean Théodore Descourtilz, from Michel Etienne Descourtilz'
Flore Pittoresque et Médicale des Antilles, Paris, 1821–9.

Fig. 2.

Fig. 1.

Fig. 3.

A. Baron del.

N. Remond imp.

Victor sculp.

Fougères.

Plate 24, *Fougères*, a hand-coloured copper engraving
from Thiébaut de Bernaud's *Traités Elémentaire
de Botanique*, Paris, 1837.

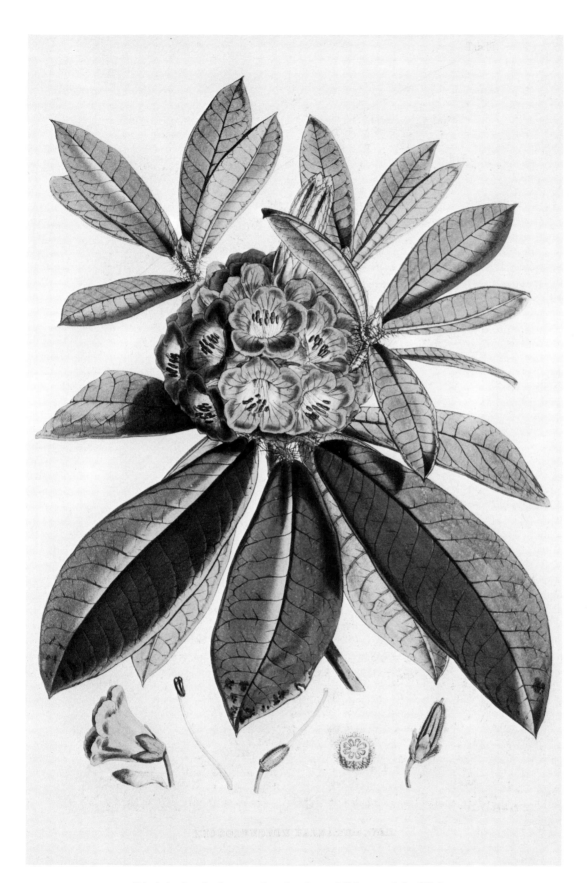

Rhododendron barbatum, a hand-coloured lithograph by Walter
Hood Fitch from Hooker's field sketch, from Joseph Dalton
Hooker's *The Rhododendrons of Sikkim-Himalaya*, London, 1849–51.

(1785–1865), who took over the direction and illustration of the *Botanical Magazine* in 1826, and in 1841 became Director of the Royal Botanic Gardens at Kew. Joseph himself edited the *Botanical Magazine* from his father's death until 1904. Between them the two Hookers produced a number of important botanical books. They were both admirably served by one of the finest of nineteenth-century flower painters, Walter Hood Fitch. Fitch excelled in painting orchids, which he produced for books by William Hooker and Bateman. Joseph Hooker's *The Rhododendrons of Sikkim-Himalaya* (1849–51) and *Illustrations of Himalayan Plants* of 1855 both have very fine hand-coloured lithographs by Fitch based on rough sketches by Indian artists. It was Joseph Hooker who, appealing to Disraeli's patriotism by showing him Fitch's excellent lithographs of the giant South American water lily (named *Victoria amazonica* after the Queen) at Kew, obtained for the artist a well-deserved state pension. Fitch's draughtsmanship is near-perfect – it is both botanically correct and very beautiful in execution – and he was his own lithographer.

Elizabeth Twining was yet another female amateur artist who produced what is, to me, perhaps the last of the great flower books. Wilfrid Blunt considers her *Illustrations of the Natural Orders of Plants* of 1849–55 botanically correct but of no aesthetic merit. I beg to disagree, and to me its 160 hand-coloured lithographs have a charm that forms a fitting finale to the history of good flower books. A great many books appeared in the mid-nineteenth century: 'Romances of Nature', 'Languages of Flowers', and the like, together with a large number of botanical and gardening magazines such as Paxton's *Magazine of Botany* and Moore's of the same name. They are often enjoyable – though unashamedly Victorian and popular in appeal – but there is not one book among them worthy of mention in the same breadth as Furber or Trew or Redouté or Thornton.

OPPOSITE Dahlias from Samuel Curtis' *The Beauties of Flora*, Gamston, Notts, 1806–20. One of the rarest of all great flower books, it has 10 plates, partly colour-printed and partly hand-coloured, from drawings by Clara Maria Pope. All but two, including this one, have landscape backgrounds, but not such fine ones as in *The Temple of Flora*.

PAGE 66 Ferdinand Bauer's hand-coloured title page to the tenth and last volume of John Sibthorp's monumental *Flora Graeca*, London, 1806–40.

PAGE 67 Plate 14, A Woodland Seat, a hand-coloured aquatint from John Buonarotti Papworth's *Ornamental Gardening*, London, 1823. This is less of a natural history book than one on gardens, but is attractive enough to merit inclusion.

PAGE 68 The Orange Pippin from Thomas Knight's *Pomona Herefordiensis*, 1811, a very good-looking book of hand-coloured aquatints of British fruit.

PAGE 69 Plate 11 from Mrs Edward Bury's *A Selection of Hexandrian Plants Belonging to the Natural Orders Amaryllidae and Liliaceae*, London, 1831–4. The plant is *Crinum pedunculatum*, and the two butterflies *Papilio Antenor* and *Papilio Menelaus*. Robert Havell engraved, printed and coloured the aquatint plates, which were partly colour-printed and party hand-coloured.

FLORA

GRÆCA

Sibthorpiana.

CENTURIÆ DECIMÆ

QUOD EXTAT.

1840.

DELPHI.

A WOODLAND SEAT.

The Orange Pippin.

EPIDENDRUM MACROCHILUM var. ROSEUM.

J.J. Jung. pinx.   Oudet. sc.

Camellia Venustissima.

Rémond. imp.

The popularization of the flower book meant, inevitably, a fall in standards. Cheaper printing methods and smaller formats meant that more people could buy flower books, but flower books that were a mere shadow of the great works of the eighteenth and early nineteenth centuries. During that period distant parts of the world were starting to be explored, and there was a ready supply of new and exciting specimens to be drawn and published. The rich were very rich, and not only did they have the money but they did not have so much to distract them as we do nowadays. The Industrial Revolution did not get a real grip on society until 1830–40. Travel was an infrequent and leisurely affair. The wealthy spent a lot of time at home, and used their money on their property, embellishing their gardens and laying them out in ever more interesting ways. Capability Brown and Humphry Repton were called in to re-design them. Books could be commissioned by kings and noblemen, or subscribed for a large sum to a few who liked to pay for them. Most of the great libraries were formed during this period and the flower book in particular benefited. The Linnaean revolution helped, of course, because it enormously assisted the international exchange of information. Fifty years or so later Mrs Loudon's *The Ladies' Flower Garden* was for the bourgeois and no longer for the aristocracy, and looks the part when put alongside Thornton or Furber, let alone Redouté. Andrews' *Flora's Gems* and *The Parterre* were books for the drawing-room, not for the library, and are the true forerunners of Victorianism. This is not intended in any way to denigrate the Victorians, but rather as a statement of fact. The grand flower book could not flourish in the boudoir, and the library, in the eighteenth-century sense, had disappeared.

Mechanical processes are very much bound up with all this. The plain, dignified copper engraving, which was responsible for many of the best flower books, continued

OPPOSITE Plate 35, *Camellia Ventustissima*, a hand-coloured
engraving after J.J. Jung from Lorenzo Berlèse's
Iconographie du Genre Caméllia, Paris, 1839–43.

PAGE 70 James Bateman's *The Orchidaceae of Mexico and Guatemala*,
London, 1837–43, is a gigantic work of which this hand-coloured
lithograph of *Epidendrum Macrochilum var. Roseum* is Plate 17.

PAGE 71 Hand-coloured lithograph from William Roscoe's
Monandrian Plants, Liverpool, 1826–9.

Plate 12, Gladioli, a hand-coloured lithograph from
Mrs J.L. Loudun's *The Ladies' Flower Garden of
Ornamental Bulbous Plants*, London, 1841.

The Mallow Tribe, drawn and lithographed by Elizabeth Twining
for her *Illustrations of the Natural Orders of Plants*,
London, 1849–55. The lithographs were all hand-coloured.

until 1830–40. But it was supplemented in the really great years by stipple, mezzotint and aquatint, the latter two processes often blended on the same plate, as in Thornton. All these were, of course, more expensive to produce. Marvellous and, again, costly colour printing was introduced, in particular in France, from 1790 to 1830. Hand-colouring or hand-finishing of coloured printed books became an art – Redouté himself put the final touches to the *grand papier* editions of his books. Lithography, invented at the end of the eighteenth century, managed to produce a few good flower books, but the process became gradually commercialized and cheapened until, with the arrival of chromolithography, an inexpensive form of printing in colours, the end came.

To sum up: the rapid exploration of the world provided the *raison d'être*, the occasion for the flower book; the wealthy and cultured patrons furnished a ready market; the mechanical processes provided the physical possibility. Perfection could not have been achieved earlier since neither the stimulus nor the craftsmanship was there; nor later, for the combination of money, interest, leisure and lack of distractions was never again present all at the same time.

ABOVE Hand-coloured lithograph of Anemones, Plate 1 of
Mary Elizabeth Rosenberg's *The Museum of Flowers*, London, 1845.

BIRDS

THE GREAT AGE OF THE BIRD BOOK came slightly later than that of the flower book, and continued until the end of the nineteenth century. Chromolithography may have spelt death to the delicacy of flowers, but gaudy parrots and humming-birds responded rather better to the technique and some very good bird books were published quite late in the Victorian era. It is a curious fact that no bird books were produced by the great Dutch flower artists of the early eighteenth century, but the high point of exploration from the point of view of collecting and drawing birds did not arrive for at least another hundred years, and the early books – from whatever country of origin – on the whole concentrated on native European birds.

Eleazer Albin's *A Natural History of Birds*, which appeared in London in three volumes from 1731 to 1738, is one of the very earliest of all comprehensive British bird books with coloured plates. Its 306 hand-coloured plates were, as the complete title tells us, '. . . Curiously Engraven from the Life, and Exactly Colour'd by the Author . . . .' All the birds depicted are native to Britain. In 1737 Albin also produced a little 12mo book called *A Natural History of English Song-Birds*, with just 23 hand-coloured engravings.

The birds in Mark Catesby's *The Natural History of Carolina, Florida and the Bahama Islands*, a large folio of 1731–43, outnumbered all the other individual categories of flora and fauna. There are 220 hand-coloured engravings in all, of which 109 are of birds. The rest are of animals, fishes, reptiles, insects and plants. This is the earliest book with coloured plates to include American birds – though printed and published in London – and to me one of the most delightful.

Catesby, born in 1679, was an Englishman who went to America for the first time in 1712 to study the flora of the New World. He was not a particularly talented artist, but his often rather naïve pictures are charming and colourful. Catesby liked to display his animals and birds in their natural habitat, and to include, where appropriate, the plants that were their source of food. Here the scientist in him tends to take over from

:Alb·in del.   Coccothraustes.

the artist, for he has a strange sense of proportion and the relative sizes of creatures and plants in some of his pictures are odd indeed! Occasionally, too, he ceases to be either naturalist or artist, and puts several creatures in unnatural juxtaposition on a single plate – something that is by no means unique to Catesby – for economy's sake.

After a second trip to America he returned to England for good in 1726, and since he lacked the necessary capital to pay other people he taught himself etching. So Catesby – traveller, artist, author, engraver and hand-colourist of the engraved plates – is another of the determined all-rounders of natural history books.

Two excellent books on European birds that appeared around this time were Johann Leonhard Frisch's *Vorstellung der Vögel in Teutschland* (German Birds Displayed), published in Berlin between 1733 and 1763, and the *Ornithologia Methodice Digesta* of Xaviero Manetti and Giovanni Gerini, better known by its Italian title *Storia Naturale degli Uccelli*, whose five large folio volumes appeared in Florence between 1767 and 1776.

ABOVE Hand-coloured engraving of a Grosbeak, Plate 56
of Eleazer Albin's *A Natural History of Birds*, London, 1731–8.
The engravings for this earliest of British bird books
with coloured plates were by Eleazar and Elizabeth Albin.

Frisch contains 255 hand-coloured engravings of a truly delightful nature, and is now very rare. It has a whole section of very jolly domestic fowl – 'tufted and top-knotted', Sacheverell Sitwell called them in *Fine Bird Books* – including the Cockerel illustrated in colour on page 91. Manetti contains 600 hand-coloured plates, each of which bears a separate dedication. This book has aroused passions of all kinds; some critics damn it outright and say that it is useless, but to the collector it is certainly a great book with very beautiful plates. It is my favourite bird book, with Frisch coming a close second. At any rate, whether it is ornithologically correct or not, it prefigured the later more ornithologically orientated books by trying, for the first time, to show birds that did not look obviously stuffed, against backgrounds that are relatively realistic ones rather than artificial branches.

The Frisch Cockerel and the Manetti Wood-Duck facing it are taken not from the original books, but from *Fine Bird Books* which came out in 1953 and is, perhaps, the nearest we shall ever get to producing a twentieth-century 'fine bird book'. The plates were superbly printed, as the five reproduced in this book will testify.

A magnificent book from Amsterdam, now rare, was Albertus Seba's *Locupletissimi Rerum Naturalium Thesauri*, whose four large folio volumes appeared between 1734 and 1765. It contains 451 hand-coloured engravings, of which 227 are of birds. Seba was a German-born apothecary practising in Amsterdam, and, like many apothecaries,

Mark Catesby's *The Natural History of Carolina, Florida and the Bahama Islands*, London, 1731–43, is the earliest book with coloured plates of American birds. This hand-coloured plate, drawn and engraved by Catesby, is of the White-Faced Teal.

Hand-coloured engraving by Pieter Tanjé, Plate 67 of
Albertus Seba's *Locupletissimi Rerum Naturalium Thesauri*, Amsterdam,
1734–65. About half the engravings in this
magnificent book are of birds, while the rest are of animals
and various curiosities from Seba's famous collection.

Hand-coloured engraving of a Cuckoo by
Jan Christiaan Sepp, from Cornelis Nozeman's
Nederlandsche Vogelen, Amsterdam, 1770–1829.

was a collector of curiosities. He himself had travelled to both the East and West Indies, and was always eager to purchase anything new and exotic brought back by sailors from voyages to distant parts of the world. His collection of fantastic oddities became internationally famous, and in 1717 he sold it for a vast sum to Peter the Great of Russia. But Seba was unable, or unwilling, to suppress his magpie instincts, and soon began another collection of curios. It was one of the essential sights of Amsterdam for Linnaeus when he visited the city, and at one point Seba even considered asking the as yet unknown naturalist to collaborate on his massive project.

The 'cabinet of curiosities' was the source for many of the illustrations in the *Locupletissimi Rerum Naturalium Thesauri*, which explains the evident lifelessness and somewhat unnatural postures of many of the subjects. Strange combinations of creatures abound in the plates. The *Thesaurus* also contained a number of freaks, such as a seven-headed hydra which was instantly denounced by Linnaeus as a fraud when he inspected the actual stuffed creature. The book is clearly of no zoological importance whatsoever, but its large number of superb plates makes it very desirable.

An excellent and more realistic Dutch book solely on birds is *Nederlandsche Vogelen*, by Cornelis Nozeman and others. Its five large folio volumes came out rather later than Seba, between 1770 and 1829. As the title states, it is restricted to native Dutch birds, of which there are 250 hand-coloured engravings by the very talented Jan Christiaan Sepp, perhaps better known for his exquisite drawings of insects.

A famous book published in England shortly before Nozeman was George Edwards' *A Natural History* of 1743–64. It came out as two separate books: *A Natural History of Uncommon Birds* appeared first, in four parts comprising four volumes, between 1743 and 1751; this was followed by *Gleanings of Natural History*, in three parts and three volumes, 1758–64. Both were quarto, and are now considered as one entity. All the plates were superbly reproduced, and there are 362 of them, all hand-coloured, in the two books taken together. The plates are unusual for having landscape backgrounds.

Another good-looking bird book, which does not seem to have attracted all the attention that it deserves, is Thomas Pennant's *The British Zoology* of 1761–6. The title is misleading, for of the 132 hand-coloured engravings 121 are of birds. Most of the drawings for the plates were made by Peter Paillou. The amateur naturalist James Bolton's *Harmonia Ruralis*, published in Halifax, England, between 1794 and 1796, is definitely not one of the great bird books, but its 80 hand-coloured plates do make it an extremely pretty and original one.

The single greatest influence on all subsequent bird and animal books must be the French polymath Buffon. Born in Burgundy in 1707, as a young man he studied law but gave it up in favour of medicine and natural history. Buffon was a prodigiously talented man whose interests and accomplishments ranged through mathematics, astronomy and all the sciences; his theories made him enemies as well as admirers.

In 1732 he visited England, where he was made a member of the Royal Society.

OPPOSITE The Purple Water Hen from George Edwards'
A Natural History, London (1st edition 1743–64).
This hand-coloured engraving is from the folio
edition, limited to 25 copies, of 1802–5. Note the landscape
background, which is unusual in natural history books.

87

A group of Finches, a hand-coloured engraving designed
and coloured by Peter Paillou, from Thomas Pennant's
The British Zoology, London, 1761–6.

James Bolton's *Harmonia Ruralis* of 1794–6 was published
at Stannary, near Halifax, England. The plates are clearly
by an amateur but they are very prettily hand-coloured;
this one is of a Canary with a nest of eggs.

Plate 90, the Little Owl, a hand-coloured engraving
from Edward Donovan's *The Natural History
of British Birds*, London, 1794–1819.

Preparations for his great work, the *Histoire Naturelle Générale*, started in 1739 when he was appointed keeper of the Jardin du Roi, the precursor of the Paris Zoo, and continued for nearly half a century until his death in 1788. Of the proposed 50 volumes, only 36 were published by the time he died. The 44 that did appear came out over a long timespan, 1749–1804, and of these there are nine (numbers 23–31) devoted to birds, which were published between 1770 and 1783. This massive undertaking covered the whole animal kingdom; in the text descriptions of the creatures were interspersed with philosophical discussions.

The *Histoire Naturelle des Oiseaux* of 1770–83 was an edited version of the nine bird volumes of the *Histoire Naturelle Générale*. The plates are from drawings by one of France's foremost bird artists at this time, François Nicholas Martinet; a Pheasant is shown in colour on page 116. The *Histoire Naturelle Générale* went into many editions, some of them very good indeed. It also influenced a large number of *suites à Buffon* (sequels) by other authors and artists.

Plate 11, a hand-coloured etching of a Lapwing from
William Hayes' *A Natural History of British Birds*,
London, 1771–5. The plate is signed in ink by
Hayes and by Gabriel Smith, the engraver.

The English Hayes family was another of those talented, artistic families, like the Sowerbys in flower painting, that continually recur in the world of natural history books. They produced a number of interesting books, of which the finest are William Hayes' *A Natural History of British Birds* of 1771–5, and *Portraits of Rare and Curious Birds . . . From Species in the Menagerie of Child, the Banker, at Osterley Park, Near London*, of 1794–9. The former title contains 40 hand-coloured etchings from drawings by Hayes and Gabriel Smith, while *Portraits of Rare and Curious Birds* contains 101 by Hayes and members of his family. The plates are often signed in ink. *Fine Bird Books*, which adopted a 'star' rating system to denote the quality of books, awarded two stars to each title, and they are certainly both very good indeed. A Red Maccaw (*sic*) – signed and dated 1779 – from *Portraits of Rare and Curious Birds* is shown in colour on page 92.

Edward Donovan produced a number of quite good books on birds, fishes and insects. *The Natural History of British Birds*, containing 244 hand-coloured engravings, came out in 10 volumes between 1794 and 1819. Other books by Donovan dealing with, or including, birds, contained fewer plates and were less important. William Lewin's *The Birds of Great Britain with Their Eggs Accurately Figured* is, in its first edition, the rarest of all English bird books. It was limited to 60 copies, in each of which all 324 of the pictures by Lewin are original paintings, and not prints – a monumental feat. The only book with which it can be compared in this sense is Mrs Bowdich's *British Fresh Water Fishes*. The *Cimelia Physica* by John Frederick Miller (who was responsible for the plates) and George Shaw was a large folio edition, published in 1796, of Miller's *Various Subjects of Natural History Wherein Are Delineated Birds, Animals and Many Curious Plants . . .* of 1776–92. Both contained 60 hand-coloured copper engravings, of which 41 are birds. Although the second edition is very much better-looking – it is larger, and the

OPPOSITE Captain Thomas Brown's *Illustrations of the American Ornithology of Alexander Wilson and Charles Lucian Bonaparte*, Edinburgh, 1831–5, was contemporary with Audubon. Hand-coloured engraving of the Honduras Turkey.

PAGES 90 AND 91 Domestic fowl in natural history plates could look just as colourful as their tropical counterparts. On the left is Plate 7, a hand-coloured engraving of a Wood Duck, from Manetti and Gerini's *Ornithologia Methodice Digesta*, Florence, 1767–76. On the right is a hand-coloured engraving of a Cockerel from Frisch's *Vorstellung der Vögel in Teutschland*, Berlin, 1733–63.

PAGE 92 Red Maccaw (*sic*), a hand-coloured etching from William Hayes' *Portraits of Rare and Curious Birds . . . at Osterley Park*, London, 1794–9. The plate is signed and dated 1779.

PAGE 93 Hand-coloured lithograph of a Red-capped Parrakeet from the best of all parrot books, Edward Lear's *Illustrations of the Family of Psittacidae or Parrots*, London, 1830–2. Lear made his own lithographs which were then printed to a very high standard by Hullmandel.

MELEAGRIS OCELLATA.
HONDURAS TURKEY.

Plate 7
Wood-Duck
[MANETTI]

Anatra d' Estate. ⊢————————⊣ *Anas Estiva.*

All'Ill.:mo Sig.:re Dottore Orazio Traversari Medico a Cervia.

W. R. R. Hayes 1779

PLATYCERCUS PILEATUS

Red-capped Parrakeet.

E.Lear delt et lithog.   Printed by C.Hullmandel.

Plate 23
Blue Jay
[AUDUBON]

Drawn from nature by J.J.Audubon F.R.S. F.L.S.

Engraved printed & Coloured by R.Havell

Blue Jay,

CORVUS CRISTATUS.

Male.1. Female.2.3.

LVIII.

PL.73.
WOODPECKERS.

TERSINA CŒRULEA
PROCNIAS NUDICOLLIS
VARIEGATUS

LONDON WATERLOW & SONS. CHROMO-LITHOGRAPHERS

typography is attractive – it is the first edition that is now very rare and therefore much sought after.

François Levaillant is one of the major figures in the history of bird books. Until overtaken by John Gould later in the nineteenth century, he was the most prolific producer of comprehensive bird books, and in sheer quality he was eclipsed only by Audubon. Born in 1753, Levaillant was a naturalist and traveller but not an artist, and in fact the books with which his name is associated have, from the point of view of the coloured plates, little to do with him. The early eighteenth century was the beginning of the period of well-planned scientific expeditions, accompanied by naturalists and sometimes also artists. Perhaps Levaillant's greatest contribution to ornithology was in the field of African birds, and the six volumes of the *Histoire Naturelle des Oiseaux d'Afrique*, published between 1796 and 1808, were – with the notable exception of books such as Merian and Catesby – among the first works produced by naturalists who had themselves travelled to unexplored parts of the world and seen these creatures in their natural surroundings.

Levaillant's accompanying text is amusing and by no means all to do with natural history; he found himself a Hottentot mistress, Nerina, after whom he later named a certain beautiful South American bird, the Nerina Trogon. He always remained the urbane French gentleman: 'He hunted the lion and leopard', Sacheverell Sitwell wrote in *Fine Bird Books*, 'in his court suit of "Blue-Boy" silk, with white gloves, ostrich-plumed hat, and lace ruffles, to show his respect for those noble animals.'

The paintings for the 300 plates in the *Histoire Naturelle des Oiseaux d'Afrique* were all done by Reinold, colour-printed and hand-finished. The great majority of the plates in Levaillant's books, however, were from drawings by Jacques Barraband, a superlative

OPPOSITE Plate 27, a colour-printed, hand-finished lithograph
of *Tersina Coerulia*, from Jean Théodore Descourtilz'
Ornitholigie Brésilienne, Rio de Janeiro, 1854–6.

PAGES 94 AND 95 Two examples of fine plates of American birds.
On the left is Plate 23, a hand-coloured aquatint of Blue Jays,
from Audubon's massive elephant folio *The Birds of America*,
London, 1827–38. The plate was engraved, printed
and coloured by Robert Havell.
On the right is a hand-coloured engraving which precedes
Audubon's plates by some years: Woodpeckers, Plate 57 of
Alexander Wilson's *American Ornithology; or the Natural History
of the Birds of the United States*, Philadelphia, 1808–14.

Plate 57, *Ramphastos Indicus*, from John Miller and
George Shaw's *Cimelia Physica*, London, 1796. Miller's contribution
was the hand-coloured copper engravings.

Le grand Cotinga.

De l'Imprimerie de Langlois.

Le grand Cotinga, a colour-printed and hand-finished
engraving from a drawing by Barraband – Plate 25 from Vol. 1
of Levaillant's *Histoire Naturelle d'une Partie d'Oiseaux
Nouveaux et Rares de l'Amériques et des Indes,*
Paris, 1801–2. The printing was by Langlois.

L'Oiseau Mouche à ventre gris. Pl. 53.

Colour-printed engraving of *L'Oiseau Mouche à Ventre Gris*,
Plate 53 of Audebert and Viellot's *Oiseaux Dorés
ou à Reflets Métalliques*, Paris, 1802. Audebert was
responsible for the plates, including their embellishment
with gold using a technique of his own invention.

Paroare Huppé.

Dessiné par Prêtre.   de l'Imprimerie de Langlois.   Gravé par Bouquet

ABOVE Plate 70, *Paroare Huppé*, a hand-coloured engraving from
Viellot's *Histoire Naturelle des Plus Beaux Oiseaux
Chanteurs de la Zone Torride*, Paris, 1805. Louis Bouquet's
engravings from Prêtre's drawings were printed by Langlois.

OVERLEAF Plate 26, a hand-coloured engraving from Bonaparte's
American Ornithology – Birds Not Given by Wilson, Philadelphia,
1825–33. The plates were by A. Rider and Titian Ramsay Peale.

Peals Egret Heron
Ardea Peala

Scolopaceus Courlan.
Aramus Scolopaceus.

Naumann's Raubvogelfalle

bird artist. Barraband had worked in a variety of environments – in the Gobelin tapestry works, and at the Sèvres porcelain factory – and had been responsible for painting the dining-room of the palace at St-Cloud. His pictures appear in the *Histoire Naturelle des Perroquets* of 1801–5 (two volumes, containing 145 engravings); in the *Histoire Naturelle des Oiseaux de Paradis* of 1801–6 (two volumes, 114 engravings); and in the *Histoire Naturelle des Promerops, des Guèpiers, et des Couroucous* (a single volume whose 85 plates came out between 1807 and 1816). All the colour-printed and hand-finished plates in these three titles were from Barraband's work, and were excellently printed, mostly by Langlois. A plate from the *Perroquets* is illustrated in colour on page 119.

The magnificence of French colour printing at this time produced a number of other superb books. The *Oiseaux Dorés ou à Reflets Métalliques* of Jean-Baptiste Audebert and Louis Jean Viellot is a beautiful work, perhaps the loveliest individual bird book of the time. As the title implies, the subjects are tropical birds, and the 190 plates had gold

ABOVE Frontispiece to Johann Naumann's *Naturgeschichte der Vögel Deutschlands*, Leipzig, 1822–60. This plate, of Naumann's Trap for Birds of Prey, is from the 2nd edition, with 396 hand-coloured engravings, of his *Naturgeschichte der Land- und Wasservögel des Nördlichen Deutschlands* (Land and Water Birds of North Germany), Leipzig and Cöthen, 1795–1817.

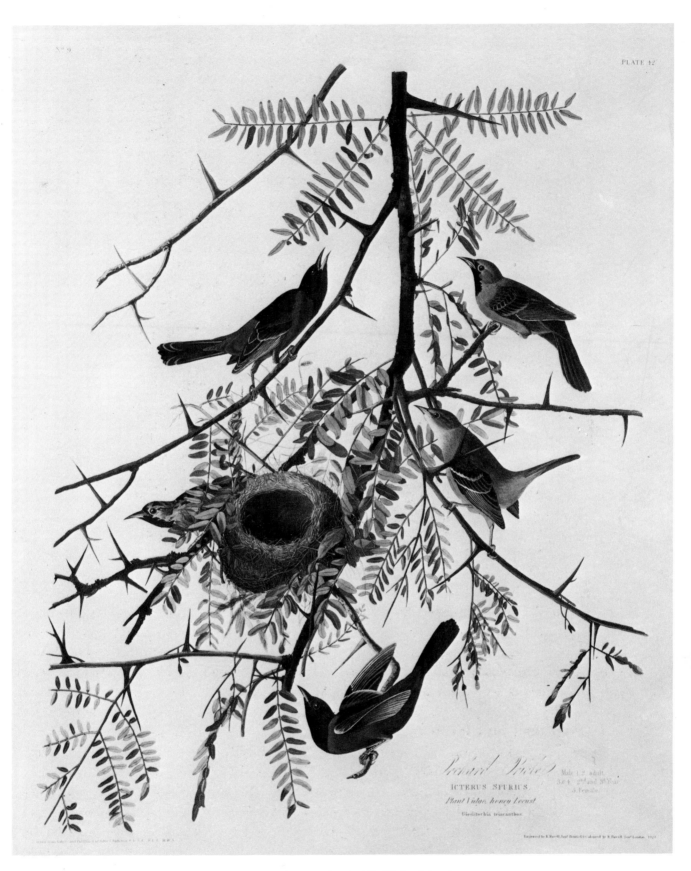

Orchard Oriole, Plate 42 of Audubon's *The Birds of America*,
London, 1827–38. With the exception of the first few,
all the hand-coloured aquatints from Audubon's watercolours
were by Robert Havell, who made a considerable contribution
to the quality of the plates.

applied to them in the re-touching – using a technique invented by Audebert – so that they look like medieval illuminations. The *Oiseaux Dorés* was always intended to be something exceptional: apart from the gold highlights on the birds, 12 copies had a gold-printed text, and a unique copy was printed all in gold, on vellum. The birds in the plates did not, of course, include any of the marvellous specimens from Australasia, which had yet to be explored; these were to be the special province of John Gould later in the century.

The *Oiseaux Dorés* came out in 1802; it was completed by Viellot after Audebert died in mid-publication. Viellot himself produced a considerable book on tropical birds in 1805 – the *Histoire Naturelle des Plus Beaux Oiseaux Chanteurs de la Zone Torride*, with 72 hand-coloured engravings by Louis Bouquet, printed by Langlois, from drawings by Jean Gabriel Prêtre. Viellot was also responsible for a number of other very good books.

American birds were represented in these years before Audubon by Alexander Wilson's *American Ornithology; or the Natural History of the Birds of the United States*, published in nine folio volumes in Philadelphia between 1808 and 1814. This, and Bonaparte's 'supplement' to it, *American Ornithology – Birds Not Given by Wilson* (four volumes, Philadelphia, 1825–33), are unusual in that they were printed and published in the United States, unlike *The Birds of America* which Audubon was to have produced and published in England.

Wilson's and Bonaparte's two books are, for obvious reasons, always considered inseparable to the bookseller, collector and bibliophile. The 76 hand-coloured plates in Wilson are not particularly exciting – compare Wilson's Woodpeckers, which are illustrated in colour on page 95, with Audubon's Blue Jays which face them – and it is the country of origin that makes it an interesting book.

Both Wilson and Bonaparte were intriguing characters. Alexander Wilson was a Lowland Scot from a poor background who, like so many others, sought a better future for himself in America. After his arrival in 1794 he turned his hand to numerous activities including teaching and various craft trades. His amateurish, passing interest in birds was encouraged by a number of friends who were genuinely interested in natural history, and an engraver, Alexander Lawson, taught him to draw. Determined to stick to some sort of occupation at last, he grew steadily more involved with American birds. He had problems with nomenclature since very few of these new birds had been properly described; the *American Ornithology* was to follow the Linnaean system.

Wilson somewhat naïvely approached Audubon, an obvious potential rival, for a subscription to the book. But perhaps he did not know that Audubon drew birds quite so well, or that he had hopes of one day publishing drawings of all the birds in America. At any rate Audubon did not sign the list, to Wilson's chagrin. Wilson undoubtedly influenced Audubon – not in style, for Audubon was a considerably more talented artist and Wilson's birds appear wooden and lifeless against Audubon's – but Wilson's

PLATE CLXXXI

ABOVE Golden Eagle, Plate 181 of *The Birds of America*. In his
original watercolour Audubon included a tiny figure of a hunter,
possibly a self-portrait, which Havell omitted from the engraving.

Great White H

PAGES 108–9 Great White Heron, Plate 281 of *The Birds of America*.
On his watercolour Audubon scribbled notes to Havell: 'Keep
closely to the Sky in depth and colouring! have the water of a
Pea-green tint.' The Florida background was probably by George Lehman.

ABOVE Yellow-Crowned Heron, Plate 336 of *The Birds of America*. In the
original watercolour the vine was painted by Maria Martin.

assiduous efforts and initiative may well have spurred Audubon on to organize his own material into a publishable form.

Charles Lucien Bonaparte was Napoleon's nephew. After 1815 he emigrated to America with his uncle Joseph, formerly King of Spain – a title Napoleon had given him when he was handing out European thrones to his relatives. Bonaparte settled in Philadelphia and became a highly respected naturalist at a very early age. He, too, met the then unknown Audubon, encouraged him to take his drawings to Europe, and tried to arrange patronage for him in Philadelphia.

Wilson and Bonaparte went into a large number of editions, as did the *Histoire Naturelle* of the great Buffon. Of the numerous *suites à Buffon* already mentioned, Coenraad Jacob Temminck's *Nouveau Recueil de Planches Coloriées d'Oiseaux*, a five-volume folio published in Paris between 1820 and 1839, is a famous example. The full title states that the book is intended to complement Buffon's coloured plates, and the 600 hand-coloured engravings are from work by Nicolas Huet and Prêtre. Temminck, like Seba in the previous century, was famous for his collection of curiosities.

Audubon, most famous of all bird artists, is really without peer. Levaillant's books are superb, being produced at the finest hour of French colour printing, and John Gould published an enormous number of very good books later in the nineteenth century, but Audubon's one great book in many ways surpasses them all.

He was born on the Caribbean island of Haiti in 1785, the illegitimate child of a French father and a Creole mother. Later, to cloud his uncertain and embarrassing origins, he perpetrated various myths, including one that he was the Dauphin, the son of Louis XVI and Marie Antoinette, who had disappeared during the French Revolution. As a young man Audubon was sent to Pennsylvania where his family had property, and became involved in a number of of unsuccessful business ventures. He had been fascinated by animals and, particularly, birds as a child in France, and had spent more time studying and drawing them than attending to other, more academic, aspects of his education.

Living now in the infant United States, most of which was quite unknown to Europeans, Audubon found himself surrounded by all sorts of new birds, and was constantly making exciting ornithological discoveries, capturing specimens, stuffing them and drawing them. Gradually he formulated what he called his 'Great Idea' – to travel extensively throughout America, and record on paper, in life size, every species of bird in the continent. His preoccupation with making the drawings life-size explains the enormous format; 'Had an ostrich or an emu been among *The Birds of America*,' Sacheverell Sitwell wrote in *Fine Bird Books*, 'Audubon would, quite likely, have increased the dimensions of his folios to include it.'

It was a Herculean task, and there were many regions of America that Audubon was never to see – he never got further west, for instance, than Galveston in Texas. But *The Birds of America*, the magnificent elephant folio that appeared between 1827 and 1838,

still contains an incredible 435 marvellous hand-coloured aquatint plates. The four
volumes were originally published in 87 parts; the first few plates were engraved by
William Lizars in Edinburgh, but after he went bankrupt Audubon engaged the
services of Robert Havell in London, who served him very well. Audubon owed a great
debt of gratitude to Havell, who improved and embellished the artist's often very rough
watercolour sketches to make them into very fine plates indeed. Audubon soon forgot
Lizars – who had, in fact, done some good work and given Audubon much assistance
during his early days in Edinburgh. But at least Havell was properly acknowledged.
After the final plates of *The Birds of America* had been printed and sent out to the
subscribers, Audubon wrote: 'The work, comprising four hundred and thirty-five
plates, and one thousand and sixty-five figures was finished on the 20th June 1838
without the continuity of its execution having been broken for a single day, and the
numbers having been delivered with exemplary regularity; for all which I am indebted
to my friend and Engraver, Mr ROBERT HAVELL.'

Audubon endured many hardships during his travels from the swamps of Florida to
the biting cold of the Atlantic coast of Canada. He suffered other financial setbacks as
well as Lizars' bankruptcy, and a setback of a different kind when a large quantity of
drawings left behind with a friend while he went off on his travels were found to have
been eaten by rats. But Audubon was nothing if not determined, and he had
considerable support in the form of Robert Havell and his own sadly neglected wife,
Lucy. In later years his two sons assisted with some of the plates – even more so for those
of *The Viviparous Quadrupeds of North America*, which will be discussed in the chapter on
animals – and various other artists, including Joseph Mason, George Lehman, and
occasionally Lucy, painted landscape backgrounds and other details.

OPPOSITE The *Oiseau-Mouche Sapho*, a colour-printed,
hand-finished plate from René Primevère Lesson's
Histoire Naturelle des Oiseaux-Mouches, Paris, 1828–30.

PAGE 114 The Roseate Cockatoo, Plate 13 of John Gould's
The Birds of Australia, London, 1840–69. The drawing and
lithograph were by Gould and Richter, and the
hand-coloured plate was printed by Hullmandel.

PAGE 115 The Stanley Crane, drawn and lithographed by
Edward Lear: Plate 14 from Gray's *Gleanings from the Menagerie
and Aviary at Knowsley Hall*, Knowsley, 1846–50.

PAGE 116 Plate 121, a Pheasant, a hand-coloured engraving from
Buffon's *Histoire Naturelle des Oiseaux*, Paris, 1770–86.

PAGE 117 *Tanagrella Rubicolla*, a coloured lithograph from the
very rare *Illustrations of the Birds of Jamaica* by
Philip Henry Gosse, London, 1849.

Pl. 27.

OISEAU-MOUCHE SAPHO.

Publié par Arthus Bertrand.

Bévalet pinx.   Rémond impr.   Coutant sculp.

J. Gould and HC Richter del et lith.

CACATUA EOS.

Hullmandel & Walton Imp.

Plate 14

STANLEY CRANE.—SCOPS PARADISEA.

Dessiné et gravé par Martinet.

Faisan, de France.

Plate LVIII.

P.H.G. del.et lith.

R.B. & R. imp.

Tanagrella ruficollis, Gmel. ♂ and ♀
(p.236)

EPIMACHUS ELLIOTI.

Premiere variété du grand Lori. Pl. 127.

Plate 32
Black-headed Tragopan
[ELLIOT]

J.Wolf & J.Smit del et lith.

CERIORNIS MELANOCEPHALA

M.&N.Hanhart imp.

He visited England and France, where he met Redouté, a number of times. The main purpose of his visits was to obtain subscriptions, then the accepted way to pre-sell such books, and it was of course in England, where he felt he would find better expertise in these matters than in America, that *The Birds of America* was engraved and published. He was an excellent self-publicist, though he certainly also made enemies, and his beguiling French accent and flowing ringlets were all part of his carefully cultivated image. His prose style, too, had a certain delightfully naïve quality – he was virtually uneducated and alway spoke rather quaint English. He had this to say about the Blue Jays illustrated in colour on page 94.

Reader, look at the plate in which are represented three individuals of this beautiful species, – rogues though they be, and thieves, as I would call them, were it fit for me to pass judgment on their actions. See how each is enjoying the fruits of his knavery, sucking the egg which he has pilfered from the nest of some innocent dove or harmless partridge! Who could imagine that a form so graceful, arrayed by nature in a garb so resplendent, should harbour so much mischief; – that selfishness, duplicity, and malice should form the moral accompaniments of so much physical perfection! Yet so it is, and how like beings of a much higher order, are these gay deceivers!

And of the White Pelican he wrote:

Ranged along the margins of the sand-bar, in broken array, stand a hundred heavy-bodied Pelicans . . . Pluming themselves, the gorged Pelicans patiently wait the return of hunger. Should one chance to gape, all, as if by sympathy, in succession open their long and broad mandibles, yawning lazily and ludicrously . . . But mark, the red beams of the setting sun tinge the tall tops of the forest trees; the birds experience the cravings of hunger . . . they rise on their

OPPOSITE The Black-Headed Tragopan from Daniel Giraud Elliot's
A Monograph of the Phasianidae or Family of the Pheasants.
An elephant folio, like Audubon, it was published in
New York, 1870–2. The plates are hand-coloured lithographs
by Joseph Wolf and Joseph Smith.

PAGE 118 *Epimachus Ellioti*, drawn and lithographed by
Joseph Wolf and Joseph Smith, from Elliot's *A Monograph
of the Paradiseidae or Birds of Paradise*, an elephant folio
published in London in 1873.

PAGE 119 *Première variété du grand Lori*, a colour-printed,
hand-finished engraving from a drawing by Barraband: Plate 127
of Leveillant's *Histoire Naturelle des Perroquets*, Paris, 1801–5.
The plates were printed by the excellent Langlois.

columnar legs, and heavily waddle to the water . . . And now the Pelicans . . . drive the little fishes toward the shallow shore, and then, with their enormous pouches spread like so many bag-nets, scoop them out and devour them in thousands.

Over the plate of the Eastern Meadowlark Audubon waxes positively lyrical:

How could I give the history of this beautiful bird, were I not to return for a while to the spot where I have found it most abundant, and where the most frequent opportunities occured of observing it? Then, reader, to those rich grass fields let us stray. We are not far from the sandy sea-shores of the Jerseys: the full beauties of an early spring are profusely spread around us; the glorious sun illumines the creation with a flood of golden light . . . .

One of the most important features of Audubon's plates is the lifelike qualities of most of the birds compared, for instance, with those of Wilson or Gould. Audubon insisted whenever possible on drawing only fresh specimens, before they stiffened and their colours faded. Some of his bird subjects do, however, look very stuffed, and these are usually found to have been specimens sent to him by others, therefore long dead by the time he drew them. The logical, if unpleasant, conclusion is that Audubon – as much sportsman as artist – killed an awful lot of birds so that we might, today, enjoy *The Birds of America*. But in those days, in a country relatively untouched by man, no one could have dreamt of today's dwindling numbers of some species, and the total extinction of others.

Contemporary with Audubon was Captain Thomas Brown's *Illustrations of the American Ornithology of Alexander Wilson and Charles Lucian [sic] Bonaparte*, produced in Edinburgh between 1831 and 1835. It contains 125 hand-coloured engravings, more primitive than Audubon's but still very pretty, of which the Honduras Turkey is illustrated in colour on page 89. The book is now rare.

René Primevère Lesson was the author of a large number of very good French bird books of the 1820s and 1830s. His *Histoire Naturelle des Oiseaux-Mouches*, published in Paris between 1828 and 1830, contained 86 plates, colour-printed and finished by hand, by the excellent Pancrace Bessa and others. The *Oiseau-Mouche Sapho* from this book is illustrated in colour on page 113. The best-known plates from Lesson's books are those of tiny exotic birds such as humming-birds and birds of paradise.

The English artist Edward Lear is better known to the general public for nonsense verses such as *The Owl and the Pussy-Cat*. But he was also a very fine landscape and bird artist who illustrated many natural history and travel books in the mid-nineteenth century.

Born in 1812, Lear was the youngest of twenty-one children, a number of whom died in infancy. As a young man he assisted Selby with the drawings for his *Illustrations of British Ornithology* of 1821–34. In 1830 he began drawing from life the parrots in the new Zoological Gardens in Regent's Park in London; these were to become the plates in his *Illustrations of the Family of Psittacidae or Parrots* of 1830–2, a large folio of 42 accurately

American White Pelican, Plate 311 of *The Birds of America*.

observed parrots which are clearly drawn from living rather than dead models. The *Platycerus Pileatus* (Red-capped Parrakeet) is illustrated in colour on page 93. The hand-coloured lithographs were executed by Lear himself, and the printer was Charles Joseph Hullmandel, one of the first English printers to produce books by lithography. Hullmandel probably also produced the first book in chromolithography, before that process became debased and ugly.

The *Parrots* were subscribed in a limited edition of 175 copies, and among Lear's subscribers was Lord Stanley (later the Earl of Derby), then President of the Zoological Society; he was to become an important patron and Lear's friend for life. The impact of the *Parrots* was considerable – on the strength of the first two parts Lear was nominated for associateship of the Linnean Society. The ornithologist William Swainson wrote to him in glowing terms: '. . . the red and yellow macaw . . . is in my estimation equal to any figure ever painted by Barraband or Audubon, for grace of design, perspective, or anatomical accuracy.' Only 12 of the projected 14 parts were ever completed.

Lear was now never short of work, and in the 1830s he was working on a number of projects – illustrations for the *Transactions of the Zoological Society*, *The Zoology of Captain Beechey's Voyage* and *The Zoology of the Voyage of HMS Beagle*. He was also preparing lithographs for his *Tortoises, Terrapins and Turtles*, which was not published until 1872.

Other employers at this time included Dr Gray of the British Museum, and the inexhaustible John Gould. Lear made some excellent bird and animal drawings for Gray's *Gleanings from the Menagerie and Aviary at Knowsley Hall*. At Lord Derby's instigation Lear went and stayed at the family seat, Knowsley Hall near Liverpool, to draw the animals and birds in the private menagerie originally set up by his father, the 12th Earl. The result was a fine series of over a hundred drawings, a number of which were to form the lithographs in Gray's *Gleanings*, a large folio of 1846–50. Gray himself was employed at the British Museum, and had been taken on by Lord Derby to write notes on the menagerie and publish them in book form. Lear was appointed curator under Gray. It was, incidentally, for the children at Knowsley that Lear started producing his now famous nonsense verses.

Lord Derby had a genuine zoological interest in his animals and did not run his menagerie as a piece of ostentatious one-upmanship, as some people did at this time. Among the Lear plates is one of an American Emu (*Rhea Americana*), and, from the following journal notes, it is clear that Lord Derby was having breeding problems with his emus and ostriches.

The six Rheas of last year are doing well, although one has somehow lost an eye [16 May 1845].
The Rhea has laid almost forty eggs, but no incubation yet [2 July 1846].
It is rather provoking our Emu will not sit, while at Wentworth their male is wanting to sit and had no eggs. John [Gray] thinks of sending our eggs to them . . . .
My only doubt about sending the Emu eggs to be hatched by the Wentworth male is, whether the carriage might not spoil them.

HELIODOXA JACULA, *Gould*

Heliodoxa Jacula, a hand-coloured lithograph from Gould's
A Monograph of the Trochilidae, or Family of Humming-Birds,
London, 1849–87. Gould and Richter lithographed their own
drawing, and the printing was done by Hullmandel and Watson.

Lord Derby seemed to have more complications over breeding waterfowl:

We have hatched three or four Goslings from a hybrid male (between the White-fronted and Bernicle) with the female of the first. John says it is a third cross, I call it a second, but at all events, how does this fact square with the principle, that mules are barren; or if not, that the fact proves the parents to be the same identical species? Surely the Bernicle and White-fronted geese cannot be said to be identical in species, any more than the Dshygetai and Burchell's Zebra, but the first has copulated with his own daughter by the last: whether she will produce is yet to be seen.

He had very little luck with his Stanley Cranes (Lear's plate of a Stanley Crane is illustrated in colour on page 115). Even if the eggs hatched, the apparently healthy chicks would always succumb to some mysterious 'cramp', which finished them off very quickly. Lear was a very fine landscape artist, too, and the plate of the Stanley Crane has a particularly lovely landscape background.

The pictures in Gould's first book, *A Century of Birds from the Himalaya Mountains*, are partly by Lear, although he is unacknowledged. He worked with Gould also on *A Monograph of the Ramphastidae or Toucans* and *The Birds of Europe*, but it was not an ideal partnership since Gould failed to appreciate the value of others. After his death Lear, not a vindictive man, was moved to write: 'In the earliest phase of his bird-drawing, he owed everything to his excellent wife & myself, – without whose help in drawing he had done nothing.'

Ironically for such a talented artist, Lear always had poor eyesight, and in 1836, still in his twenties, he wrote that his eyes were so bad, 'that no bird under an ostrich shall I soon be able to do'. By 1846, however, he had become so well established that he was summoned to give drawing lessons to Queen Victoria, but although his talent was evident and he became highly successful and sought after, he never made very much money for himself.

Philip Henry Gosse's delightful *Illustrations of the Birds of Jamaica*, a plate from which is reproduced in colour on page 117, is now very rare. It came out as a small quarto with 52 lithographs in 1849. Another book on exotic birds from this part of the globe was Jean Théodore Descourtilz' *Ornithologie Brésilienne*, a large folio with 48 hand-coloured lithographs by Descourtilz; Plate 27, *Tersina Coerulia*, is illustrated in colour on page 96. The book was published in Rio de Janeiro in 1854–6. This, and Descourtilz' earlier *Oiseaux Brillans du Brésil*, published in Paris in 1834, are among the very few books with coloured plates on South American birds.

It is fitting that this chapter on birds should finish with two of the very best, and also most prolific, of bird artists: John Gould and Daniel Giraud Elliot. Gould, born in 1804, is not for nothing universally known as 'the Bird Man'. His output was prodigious, all in folio format, and he directed or participated in most of the activities involved, from obtaining the specimens to drumming up subscriptions. Among the

ACCIPITER NISIS.

ABOVE *Accipiter Nisis*, the Sparrow-Hawk, a hand-coloured lithograph
from John Gould's *The Birds of Great Britain*, London, 1862–73.
The drawing and lithography were by Joseph Wolf and Henry Constantine Richter.

OVERLEAF *Argusianus Grayii*, a hand-coloured lithograph
from a drawing by Joseph Wolf and Joseph Smit, from
Daniel Giraud Elliot's *A Monograph of the Phasianidae
or Family of the Pheasants*, New York, 1870–2.

GRAYII.

CINNYRIS MARIQUENSIS

Cinnyris Mariquensis, a hand-coloured lithograph from
George Shelley's *A Monograph of the Nectariniidae (Cinnyridae)*,
or Family of Sun-Birds, London, 1876–80.
The lithographs were all by John Gerrard Keulemans.

artists he employed – apart from Lear – were his wife and Joseph Wolf. Wolf was a German-born painter who produced some splendid work that has been put in the same class as Audubon and Lear. Most of his drawings were done in England, where he died in 1899. Hullmandel printed Gould's books, and they represent some of the best examples of lithography ever produced.

Gould was a taxidermist by profession, and his first book was the result of acquiring a collection of Himalayan bird skins; his wife, previously untrained in the skill, lithographed Gould's own drawings, and when he was unable to find a publisher he brought it out at his own expense. The result was *A Century of Birds from the Himalaya Mountains* of 1831–2.

Gould's books were highly successful, but the supply of birds for more books – or to continue unfinished ones – began to dwindle. So he decided, in 1838, to visit Australia himself to gather more specimens for *The Birds of Australia*. (Two parts of this venture had already appeared, but it was abandoned at this point, and the existing plates incorporated into the new *Birds of Australia*, begun after his return in 1840. The first version is the rarest of all Gould's books.) An artist called Henry Constantine Richter was taken on to make drawings for the new *Birds of Australia* – Richter's Roseate Cockatoo, Plate 13 of that book, is shown in colour on page 114. Richter's arrangement of the birds, often in some sort of background, was always pleasing, but his birds do look rather stuffed when compared, for instance, with those of Audubon.

For sheer numbers of very good books Gould is unchallenged. *The Birds of Europe* (1832–7), *A Monograph of the Ramphastidae* (1833–5), *A Monograph of the Trogonidae* (1836–8), *A Monograph of the Trochilidae* (1849–87), *The Birds of Asia* (1830–83), *The Birds of Great Britain* (1862–73), and *The Birds of New Guinea and the Adjacent Islands* (1875–88), all merit three stars in *Fine Bird Books*! Gould was particularly fond of monographs, and some of them took practically a lifetime for the last of their plates to appear. He loved brightly coloured birds, and so did his public; lithography was admirably suited to them.

Gould and his team worked in rather chaotic, overcrowded conditions from his house in Charlotte Street, London. Boxes of dead birds were continually being delivered; Sacheverell Sitwell visualized it thus in *Fine Bird Books*: 'This is the house of the greatest figure in bird illustration after Audubon. Every room is full of the bodies of birds; there are bird skins on every table; and every spare foot of space is given over to the lithographic presses and the hand-colouring.' After Gould's death a bookseller bought the copyright in the remaining plates in the house; boxes and boxes were taken away, and some of them were not opened for another half-century, when plates that had been published a hundred years before were discovered as bright and colourful as if they had been printed yesterday.

The works of the American Daniel Giraud Elliot, along with the *Birds of Paradise* of Bowdler Sharpe, mark the end of the period of great bird books. Elliot's *Monograph of the*

Paradiseidae of 1873 contains 37 hand-coloured lithographs from drawings by Joseph Wolf and Joseph Smith. The *Monograph of the Paradiseidae*, published in Edinburgh, is a handsome book but ornithologically less interesting than Bowdler Sharpe's, which came out in 1891–8, by which time considerably more species had been discovered.

Elliot's *Monograph of the Phasianidae* came out a little earlier, in 1870–2. It has 81 hand-coloured lithographs by Wolf and Smith, and is interesting in that, unlike the *Paradiseidae*, it was published in New York. Both books are elephant folios. Plates from the *Paradiseidae* and the *Phasianidae* are illustrated in colour on pages 118 and 120 respectively.

The *Monograph of the Phasianidae* was the last of the really good bird books. Other attractive, though less important books, were to appear, such as Shelley's *Monograph of the Nectariniidae . . . Or Family of Sun-Birds* of 1876–80, but certainly after the end of the century, with the decline of chromolithography, no more really good bird books were published.

ANIMALS AND FISH

ANIMAL BOOKS, as explained in the Introduction, have alway been rather less interesting than flower and bird books, and less popular among collectors of natural history books. There are exceptions, of course, but animals seem to have been a less inspiring subject for artist and engraver; Audubon's book on animals, for instance, *The Viviparous Quadrupeds of North America*, is not a patch on *The Birds of America*. One irrefutable reason is that birds, flowers and butterflies are considerably more colourful than animals. Looking through many animal books, or those parts of larger, more comprehensive works that deal with animals, one is struck by the uniformity of colour – predominantly brown – in the plates. We cannot complain, for certainly both predators and prey in the animal world need camouflage, and they do not exist for the benefit of the connoisseur of fine books. But it does mean that rather different criteria have to be adopted when selecting animal books with coloured plates. Edward Lear's gift for reproducing the texture of a monkey's fur, for example, makes him a very fine animal artist indeed, but we miss the brilliant plumage of his parrots. Mountain sheep in Audubon's folios lack, in spite of background of mountain scenery, the spectacular attraction of his flamingoes or pelicans.

Among the earliest good books in the period 1700–1900 to include animals was Mark Catesby's *The Natural History of Carolina, Florida and the Bahama Islands* of 1731–43. Half of Catesby's own hand-coloured engravings are of birds, and the remaining 111 include exotic fish and some splendid and particularly lifelike snakes, two of which are illustrated in colour on pages 142 and 143. Snakes are for obvious reasons disliked by very many people, but these two very colourful examples have a certain appeal and Plate 58, the Wampum Snake with a Red Lily, seems to have come straight from the Garden of Eden. Catesby explained that the snake had received its strange name 'from the resemblance it has to *Indian* money called *Wampum*, which is made of shells cut into regular pieces, and strung with a mixture of blue and white . . . .'

OVERLEAF *Trigla volitans*, the Flying Fish, a hand-coloured
engraving from Marcus Elieser Bloch's *Ichtyologie
ou Histoire Naturelle des Poissons*, Berlin, 1782–95
(German edition), and 1785–97 (French edition,
from which this plate is taken).

Gestochen auf Kosten des

TRIGLA VOLITANS.
Der fliegende Seehahn.
L'Arondel de Mer.
The Flying-Fish.

ser Orden-Agenten Herrn v. Cobres in Augsburg. 351.

J. F. Hennig fc.

The text – unusually for a natural history book – is delightfully written and tells us many curious things about America and its native inhabitants at that time. Of the Green-Snake, Plate 57, Catesby has this to say: 'This inoffensive little Snake abides among the branches of trees and shrubs, catching flies and other insects, on which they feed: . . . They are easily reclaimed from their wildness, becoming tame and familiar, and are very harmless, so that come people will carry them in their bosoms.' The plant on which the snake is coiled is *Caffena vera Floridanorum*, Catesby tells us, and he goes on to explain that it was greatly esteemed by the Indians, who would make a decoction of the leaves, 'which they drink in large quantities, as well for their health as with great gust and pleasure . . . . They have an annual custom in the spring of drinking it with ceremony; the inhabitants assemble at the Town-house, having previously by fire purged their houses of all their old furniture . . . .' Then, in order of seniority, starting with the king and ending with the women and children, they purged themselves with what Catesby calls 'this emetick broth'. 'They say', he ends, 'it restores lost appetite, strengthens the stomach, giving them agility and courage in war, &c.' It seems to have had all the features of a Victorian cure-all!

An early and quite amazing book on fishes is Louis Renard's *Poissons, Ecrevisses et Crabes*, a folio published in Amsterdam in 1718–19. Its 100 brilliantly hand-coloured plates are very unusual. The only fish book with it can be compared for the colourfulness of its plates is Marcus Elieser Bloch's *Ichtyologie ou Histoire Naturelle, Générale et Particulière des Poissons*, perhaps the most famous and certainly the most remarkable of all books on fish. A plate from the 1754 edition of Renard's book is illustrated in colour on page 139, with one from Bloch opposite it.

The original edition of Block was published in German, between 1782 and 1795, as

---

OPPOSITE Plate 9, *Sciurus brachyotus*, a squirrel from
East Africa, from Christian Gottfried Ehrenberg's
Symbolae Physicae, Berlin, 1828–45.
The plates were a mixture of copper engravings and lithographs;
the drawing for this one was made by F. Bürde.

PAGE 138 Two remarkable books on fish.
Above, Marcus Elieser Bloch's *Ichtyologie ou Histoire Naturelle
et Générale des Poissons*, Berlin, 1785–97, contains marvellous
hand-coloured plates, some embellished with silver and gold.
This is Plate 323, *Anthias Formosus* (the Grunt).
Below, Mrs Sarah Bowdich's *The Freshwater Fishes of Great
Britain Drawn and Described*, London, 1828, is almost unique
in that its pictures are original watercolours, not prints.
This illustration is of the Trout.

PAGE 139 Plate 4, a typically brilliant hand-coloured
engraving from Louis Renard's *Poissons, Ecrévisses et Crabes*,
Amsterdam, 1754. It is perhaps the most fantastic
book, in all senses, on fish.

PAGES 140–1 Aquatint of an Angora Goat from Charles Catton's
Animals Drawn from Nature and Engraved, London, 1788.

SCIURUS brachyotus

Habessinia.

ANTHIAS FORMOSUS.

Gestochen auf Kosten Sr. Excel. des wirklich Etats-Ministers Herrn v. Struensee.

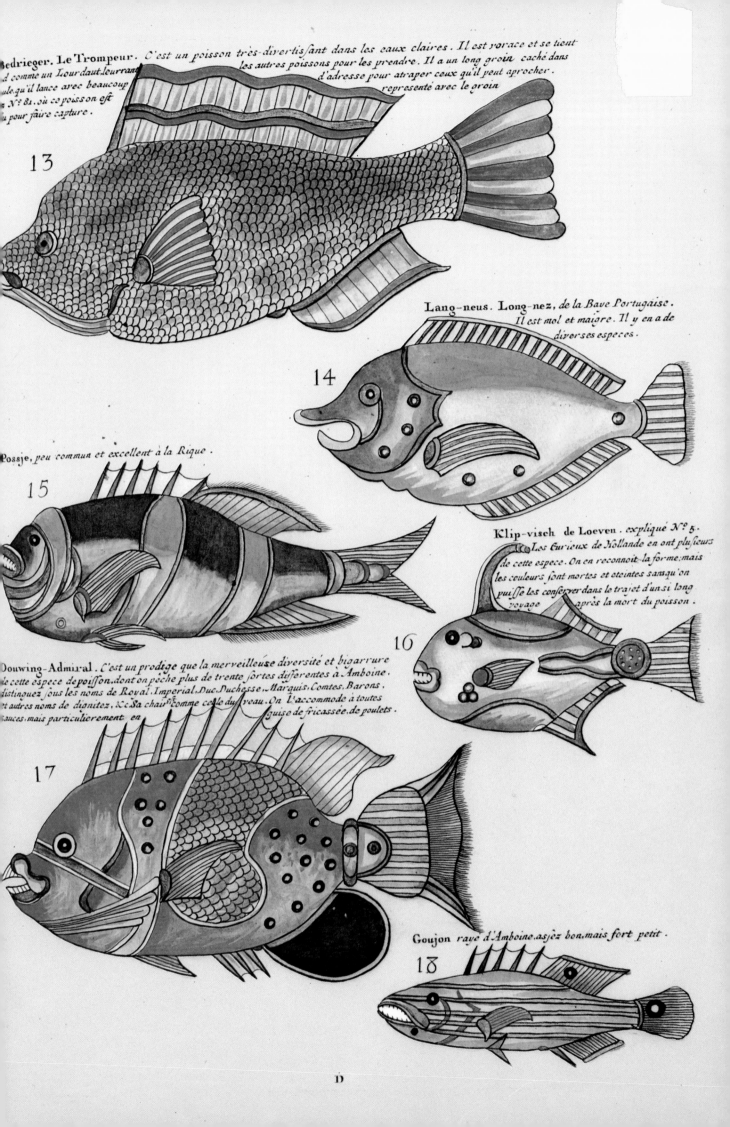

Bedrieger. Le Trompeur. C'est un poisson très-divertissant dans les eaux claires. Il est vorace et se tient
d comme un Lourdaut. leurrant les autres poissons pour le prendre. Il a un long groin caché dans
ule qu'il lance avec beaucoup d'adresse pour atraper ceux qu'il peut aprocher.
N.º 81. où ce poisson est représenté avec le groin
u pour faire capture.

13

Lang-neus. Long-nez, de la Baye Portugaise.
Il est mol et maigre. Il y en a de
diverses especes.

14

Possje, peu commun et excellent à la Rique.

15

Klip-visch de Loeven. expliqué N.º 5.
Les Curieux de Hollande en ont plusieurs
de cette espece. On en reconnoit la forme, mais
les couleurs sont mortes et eteintes sansqu'on
puisse les conserver dans le trajet d'un si long
voyage après la mort du poisson.

16

Douwing-Admiral. C'est un prodige que la merveilleuse diversité et bigarrure
de cette espece de poisson, dont on pêche plus de trente sortes differentes à Amboine.
distinguez sous les noms de Royal. Imperial. Duc. Duchesse. Marquis. Comtes. Barons.
et autres noms de dignitez. &c Sa chair comme celle du veau. On l'accommode à toutes
sauces, mais particulierement en guise de fricassée. de poulets.

17

Goujon rayé d'Amboine. assez bon, mais fort petit.

18

THE

Drawn from Nature Engrav'd & Published by Chas Catton Jun

RA GOAT.

N.º on the Terrace Tottenham Court Road March 1 1755

Anguis &c.

Cassena &c.

Lilium &c.   Anguis &c.

Tab. IX.

A. J. Röfel fec. et exc.

Allgemeine Naturgeschichte der Fische, but a French-language edition of 12 volumes, with 432 beautiful hand-coloured plates, some heightened in silver and gold, was published in Berlin between 1785 and 1797, so the two works are in fact contemporary. The names of the fish are given on the plates in several languages, and the inclusion of Latin names ensured that any language problem would be overcome. There is no text. Some of the plates are dedicated, below the fish, to different patrons – aristocrats and learned societies, for instance; there is not beating about the bush: each dedication clearly states that the person or persons mentioned paid for that particular plate to be engraved!

The German Augustin Roesel von Rosenhof's *Historia Naturalis Ranarum*, a folio produced in Nuremberg in 1758, contains 48 splendid coloured plates that should delight everyone, frog-lovers or not. *Rana arborea*, a Tree Frog, is illustrated in colour on page 144. Many of the plates show the various stages in the development of frogs, from spawn through to adult. Roesel von Rosenhof also produced a very attractive book on insects which is discussed and illustrated in the following chapter.

Domestic animals were excellently portrayed in England in Charles Catton's *Animals Drawn from Nature and Engraved, with a Description of Each Animal*, of 1788, and, fifty years later, by David Low's *The Breeds of the Domestic Animals of the British Islands* of 1842, which, although it is a natural history book, seems also to be part of the great English tradition of landscape painting. Plates from both books are shown in colour on pages 140–1 and 170–1. Catton has 36 coloured aquatints with enjoyable backgrounds. Low's book is a two-volume folio with 56 coloured plates. Low, Professor of Agriculture at Edinburgh University, wrote extensively on agricultural subjects. It is perhaps the best book of its kind and must appeal to many who, like me, are not hard-core naturalists.

OPPOSITE *Rana arborea*, a Tree Frog: Plate 9 from
Roesel von Rosenhof's *Historia Naturalis Ranarum*, Nuremberg,
1758. Both the drawings and the hand-coloured copper
engravings made from them were by Roesel von Rosenhof.

PAGES 142 AND 143 Two colourful snakes from Vol. 11 of
Mark Catesby's *The Natural History of Carolina, Florida and
the Bahama Islands*, London, 1731–43. The hand-coloured
engravings were made by Catesby himself, from his own drawings.
On the left, Plate 57 shows the Green-Snake coiled on a
branch of *Caffena vera Floridanorum*.
Plate 58, on the right, is of the Wampum-Snake with a Red Lily.

A decorative hand-coloured copper engraving from
Roesel von Rosenhof's *Historia Naturalis Ranarum*, Nuremberg, 1758.

A number of attractive books on fish came out in the nineteenth century, though they vary considerably in style and quality according to the time at which they were produced. Audubon, visiting London in the late 1830s to obtain subscriptions for *The Birds of America*, wrote bitterly to his friend John Bachman: 'Insects, reptiles and fishes are now the rage, and these fly, swim or crawl . . . in every Bookseller's window.'

Edward Donovan, author of several books covering different aspects of natural history, published between 1802 and 1806, in five octavo volumes with 120 coloured plates, his *Natural History of British Fishes*. Mrs Sarah Bowdich's *The Freshwater Fishes of Britain Drawn and Described* is a very special kind of book. A quarto, published in 1828 by the famous engraver and printer Ackermann, it has 47 original drawings – not prints. Almost all are coloured. It is a very fine book, though not quite in the same class as Bloch, whose large folio size makes it rather more imposing. A Bowdich plate is illustrated in colour on page 138. John Whitchurch Bennett's *The Most Remarkable and Interesting Fishes Found On the Coast of Ceylon*, a quarto produced in 1830, contains 30 hand-coloured plates which are so lovely that it is one of my favourite old natural history books on any subject.

Three important books on mammals from the first half of the nineteenth century are the *Histoire Naturelle des Mammifères* of Geoffroy St-Hilaire and Cuvier, Ehrenberg's *Symbolae Physicae*, and Audubon and Bachman's *The Viviparous Quadrupeds of North America*. Baron Cuvier, known as the 'dictator of biology', was the author of the famous and monumental *Le Règne Animal* of 1836–49. One of the greatest naturists and palaeontologists of his age, he enjoyed a tremendous reputation in his native France and abroad. The *Histoire Naturelle* came out in both a four- and a seven-volume edition between 1818 and 1842, and contains 430 or 432 plates.

Christian Gottfried Ehrenberg's *Symbolae Physicae* was published in Berlin between 1828 and 1845. It is a large folio dealing with creatures from northern and eastern Africa. Plate 9, a squirrel from 'Habessinia' (Ethiopia to the modern reader) is illustrated in colour on page 137. Ehrenberg travelled widely in the Middle East and parts of Asia. Another German book on animals published about this time was Johann Schreber's work on mammals, *Die Säugthiere in Abbildungen nach der Natur*, a quarto volume produced in Leipzig between 1804 and 1810 (dating is difficult, since even Nissen's standard bibliography of animal books is confusing on this point). The book contains 38 coloured plates.

The Viviparous Quadrupeds of North America is an interesting book, but smaller than *The Birds of America* – it is a folio – and it certainly lacks the dramatic impact of the *Birds*. One of the reasons, apart from the simple one that American birds are more brightly coloured than American mammals, is that the plates are not all from Audubon's work. Although other artists had certainly assisted him with landscape backgrounds, vegetation and other details in the drawings for *The Birds of America*, whole plates in the *Quadrupeds* are the work of his collaborators; they included John Bachman, his

OVERLEAF Plate 109, the Pike, a hand-coloured engraving from
Edward Donovan's *The Natural History of British Fishes*, London, 1802–6.

PAGES 150–1 Plate 2, a hand-coloured engraving from
John Whitchurch Bennett's *The Most Remarkable and Interesting
Fishes Found On the Coast of Ceylon*, London, 1830.

London Pub.d as the Act directs

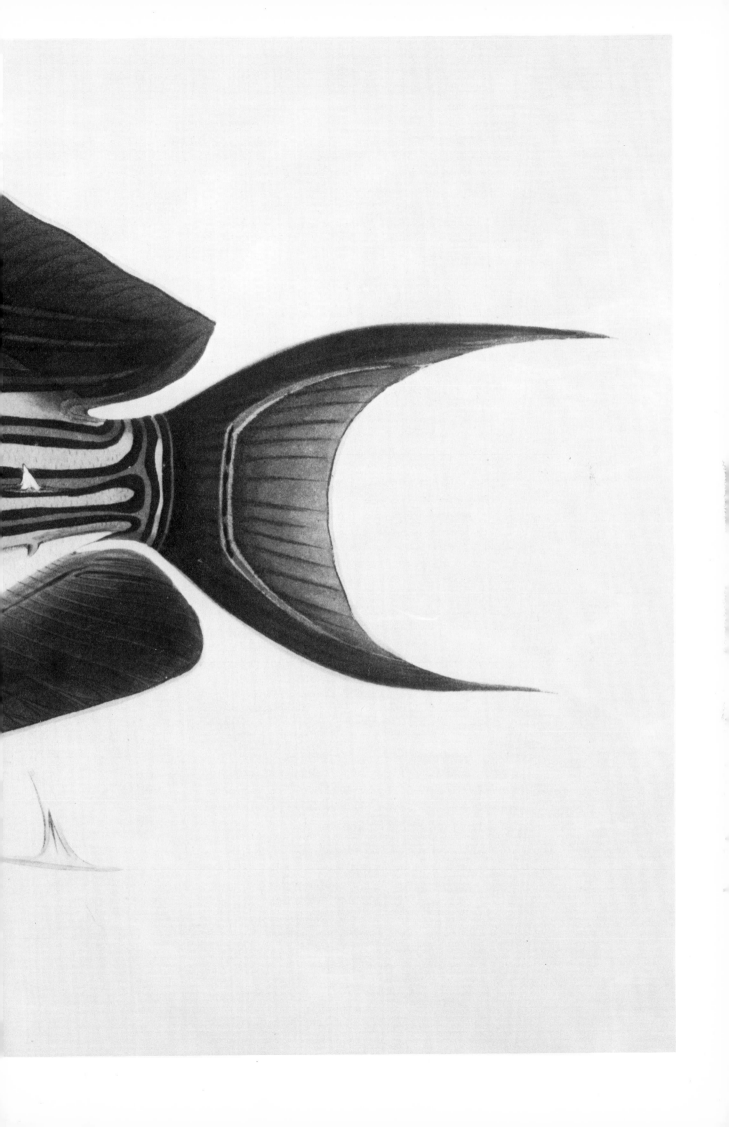

Lithog de C. de Last

...ale.

co-author, and his sons, Victor and John Woodhouse. Although they were perfectly good artists, they were not up to Audubon's own standards. Another reason is the difference in printing methods – the plates in *The Birds of America* are all aquatints, while those in the *Quadrupeds* are lithographs. The three-volume folio with its 150 hand-coloured lithographs by J.T. Bowen of Philadelphia appeared between 1845 and 1848 in New York. A smaller (large octavo) edition, called simply *The Quadrupeds of North America*, with and additional five plates, was published by Victor Audubon in 1849–54. A Polar Bear by John Woodhouse Audubon is shown in colour on page 172.

Audubon had first met his collaborator on the *Quadrupeds* in the early 1830s. The Rev. John Bachman was a Lutheran minister from Charleston, South Carolina; he had a strong interest in natural history and a lifelong friendship developed between the two men. From the start Audubon did not display the same perseverance over the *Quadrupeds* as he had over *The Birds of America* – perhaps because he preferred birds, or perhaps because he was now older (he was fifty-seven when he started work on it) – and Bachman, trying hard to write the text to accompany the plates, despaired in particular of trying to prise information on the various creatures' habits out of Audubon. Bachman, who knew about animals, warned him that it would be no easy task, that Audubon would have to find many of the species for himself since they were either unknown or at any rate undocumented, and that many of them were so similar as to be highly confusing to the naturalist. In 1843 Audubon led a small party on an expedition to the Rockies to gather material. They never reached the Rockies, but returned home with large quantities of specimens pickled in rum – enough animals to satisfy Bachman. By 1848 the last of the plates had appeared; Audubon, worn out by the hardships of a strenuous life, lived only another three years.

There are, of course, many examples of animals among the plates of *The Birds of America* – notably small mammals, which are the food of many birds of prey and were therefore suitable accompaniments to plates of owls, for instance. The squirrel in Plate 66 of *The Birds of America* was originally painted by Audubon as a separate watercolour and added to the owl by Robert Havell, when he was engraving the plate, to improve the composition. The squirrel appeared again in one of the plates in the *Quadrupeds*. Audubon's speciality in the *Quadrupeds* was small mammals, and many of these were his work rather than that of his sons. One of the most famous of the plates in *The Birds of America* is Plate 21, a rattlesnake attacking a mocking-bird's nest. Audubon was severely criticized for this, since it was believed by many naturalists at that time that rattlesnakes did not climb trees and that their fangs curled only inwards (Audubon was in fact right on both scores!). The snake, though putrefying in the Louisiana heat long before Audubon had put the finishing touches to his painting, is remarkably lifelike, and the whole thing is a tribute to his remarkable powers of observation.

A slightly later book on American Fauna was John Cassin's *Mammalogy and Ornithology*.

PAGES 152–3 Hand-coloured lithograph of a Leopard from
Geoffroy St-Hilaire and Cuvier's *Histoire Naturelle des
Mammifères*, Paris, 1818–42. The original drawing
was by J.C. Werner.

Galeopithecus variegatus Geoffr.

ABOVE *Galeopithecus*, the Flying Lemur, a hand-coloured
engraving from Johann Christian Schreber's *Die Säugthiere
in Abbildungen nach der Natur*, Leipzig, 1804–10.

OVERLEAF **Plate** 73, *Ovis Montana*, the Rocky Mountain Sheep,
from Audubon and Bachman's *The Viviparous Quadrupeds of
North America*, New York, 1845–8. The original drawing
for the hand-coloured lithograph was done by Audubon.

Drawn from Nature by J.J.Audubon F.R.S.F.L.S

PLATE LXXIII.

TANA, DESM

AIN SHEEP.

Emys insculpta.

13.

Plate 13, *Emys insculpta*, a hand-coloured lithograph
from John Edwards Holbrook's *North American Herpetology*, Philadelphia, 1842.

United States Exploration Expedition under Charles Wilkes, a folio published in Philadelphia in 1858. It has no text. Its 42 coloured plates, from drawings by T.R. Peale, are mostly of birds, which are more colourful than the animals; these are generally very monochrome in effect, being for the most part brown, in uncoloured landscape backgrounds. The expedition in question lasted from 1838 to 1842, under the command of Charles Wilkes of the United States Navy, who also explored Antarctica as part of this voyage.

John Edwards Holbrook's *North American Herpetology* dealt with the reptile life of the North American continent. Its five quarto volumes appeared in Philadelphia between 1836 and 1840, with 115 coloured lithographs. The second, and better, edition of 1842 is the one illustrated here. Holbrook's book was scientifically orientated and he took pains to ensure the accuracy of his information, both verbal and pictorial. In his Preface he wrote: 'The colouring of the plates may be fully relied on, as almost every one was done from life; and when coloured from dead animals, it is always mentioned in the description, so that no one may be deceived.' Holbrook was absolutely scrupulous about this. At one time he was given some previously unknown specimens obtained in the newly opened Oregon Territory. Most naturalists would have been thrilled and only too eager to include them among their plates, but because pickling in alcohol had caused the specimens to fade badly Holbrook decided not to include them among the coloured plates of the *North American Herpetology*, but published them uncoloured, in an academic journal.

Certain types of flora and fauna involve the naturalist in more discomfort and hardship than others – catching and drawing spiders in the South American jungle, for instance, would be a considerably more hazardous task than tracking down the humble thrush in Europe. Holbrook vividly describes the problems faced by the collector of reptiles:

The science [of] Herpetology has been more neglected than all other branches of zoology; for the study of Reptiles offers difficulties more numerous and insurmountable than those presented by any other class of vertebrated animals. Inhabiting, for the most part, deep and extensive swamps, infested with malaria, and abounding with diseases during the summer months, when Reptiles are most numerous, time is wanting to observe their modes of life with any prospect of success. Regarded, moreover, by most persons as objects of detestation, represented as venomous, and possessed of the most vigorous properties, few have been hardy enough to study their character and habits.

In spite of all this Holbrook himself was clearly undeterred by malarial mosquitoes and the unpleasant prospect of snakebite.

The English artist Edward Lear's part in Gray's *Gleanings from the Menagerie and Aviary at Knowsley Hall* of 1846–50 has already been discussed in some detail in the chapter on birds. Although most of Lear's plates are of birds, the first few are of animals. Plate 1, the

OVERLEAF Black-Footed Ferret, from Audubon and Bachman's
The Quadrupeds of North America, New York, 1849–54.
The original drawing was by John Woodhouse Audubon.

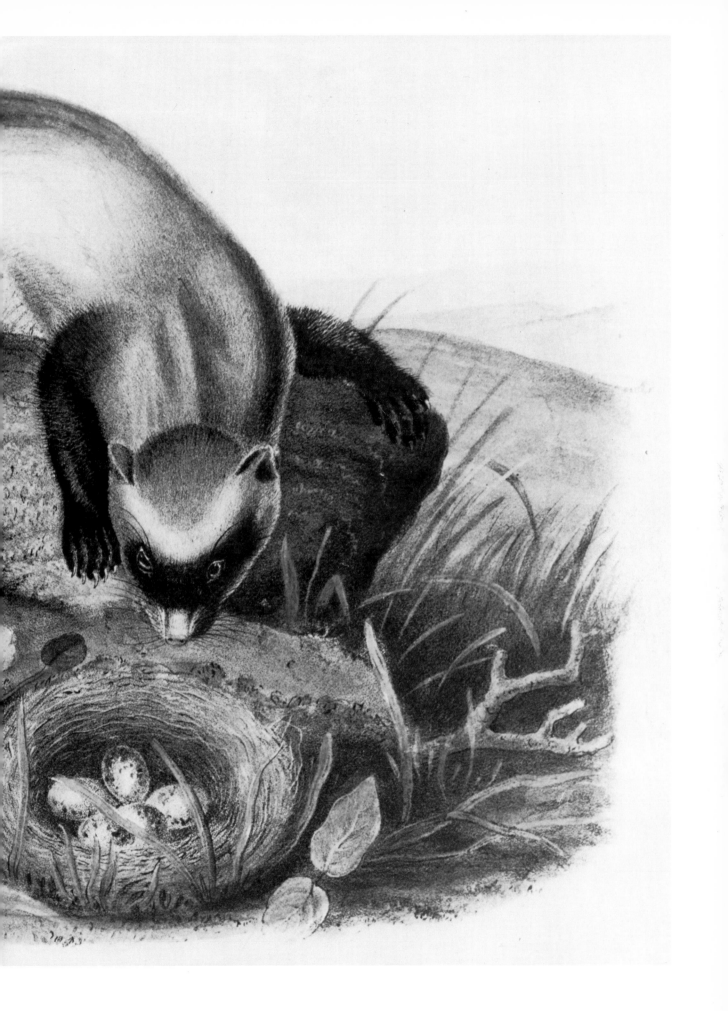

ABOVE Plate 66 from Audubon's *The Birds of America*,
a hand-coloured aquatint of a Barred Owl about to pounce on a
Grey Squirrel, is a typical example of a bird plate
into which Audubon has introduced small mammals.

OPPOSITE *Cervus macrotis*, a Stag, a coloured engraving
from a drawing by Titian Ramsay Peale, from John Cassin's
*Mammalogy and Ornithology. United States Exploration
Expedition under Charles Wilkes*, Philadephia, 1858.

Cervus macrotis. Say.

OVERLEAF The Ielerang or Javan Squirrell (*sic*), *Sciurus Javanensis*,
a hand-coloured lithograph by J.W. Moore after
a drawing by Edward Lear, from Gray's *Gleanings from the
Menagerie and Aviary at Knowsley Hall*, Knowsley, 1846–50.
Hullmandel and Watson printed the plates for this book.

E. Lear del.

IELERANG OR JAV

SCIURUS JAVENSIS

J.W Moore lithog

Plate 6

Vitoe, is shown in colour opposite. The texture of the fur and the brightness of the creature's eyes show what a very good artist Lear was.

By far the larger quantity of the plates in Gray's *Gleanings* – those in the second volume, entitled *Hoofed Quadrupeds* – are by another artist, B. Waterhouse Hawkins. He was less talented than Lear and his deer, in particular, have a sentimental, anthropomorphic quality, but the plates are interesting for showing exotic animals in captivity – though with an attempt to place them in a rudimentary indigenous background, such as a desert landscape, where appropriate! Writing to Gray, Lord Derby told him that the llama was easier to keep than its relations the guanaco, the alpaca and the vicuna. He regarded it as a gentle-natured creature, but thought its wool was 'unfit for finer fabrics'. He had more problems with vicunas and alpacas. Alpaca wool was at that time very popular for clothing, but, he wrote, 'The length of the voyage, added to unskilful treatment, so much impairs the health of those that survive, that they seldom live for any length of time after their arrival; otherwise they could, with judicious treatment, in all possibility be naturalized . . . .'

William Houghton's *British Freshwater Fishes*, folio, 1879, is a relatively late Victorian book on fish. It has 40 coloured lithographs and is also embellished with pleasant little uncoloured landscape engravings of the parts of Britain in which the various fish are to be found. Houghton, a Shropshire clergyman, aimed his book at the fisherman rather than the naturalist, and the text (of which there is, unusually, plenty) gives information about recognition, feeding and breeding habits, habitat, bait and so on. Among his hints on catching grayling he offers the following useful information:

Mr Francis says that 'the most slaughtering way of fishing for Grayling is with the grasshopper'.

PAGES 166–7 Plate 51, Llamas, from Part II (*Hoofed Quadrupeds*)
of Gray's *Gleanings*. The drawings for the hand-coloured
lithographs were by B. Waterhouse Hawkins.

OPPOSITE The Vitoe, drawn and lithographed by Edward Lear:
Plate I of Gray's *Gleanings from the Aviary and Menagerie at
Knowsley Hall*, Knowsley, 1846–50.
The lithographs were printed by Hullmandel.

PAGES 170–1 One of the finest books on domestic animals is
David Low's *The Breeds of the Domestic Animals of the
British Islands*, London, 1842. Among its 57 coloured
lithographs is this magnificent Chillingham Bull.

Plate 1

VITOE.—NYCTIPITHECUS INFULATUS.

Hullmandel & Walton Lithographers

WILD OR W

Bull, from Chillingham P

PROFESSOR LOW'S ILLUSTRAT

London Published April

EST BREED.

S OF THE DOMESTIC ANIMALS.

Longman. Paternoster Row.

On Stone by Wm E. Hitchcock

Drawn from Nature by J W Audubon

Polar Bear

Lith Printed & Col^d by J T P

The grasshopper, so called, is not a grasshopper at all, and though actually an artificial bait, in no wise resembles a grasshopper; why it should have been called a grasshopper any more than a gooseberry, which it much more resembles, I cannot conceive. No matter: this is the grasshopper.

The criteria for selecting books and plates have not been primarily those of zoological interest or scientific merit, yet there is an over-riding reason for referring to Charles Darwin here. His influence on naturalists in the second half of the nineteenth century was immense. In this sense we can consider him in the same context as Linnaeus – not so much actually part of the story from the point of view of the book-lover, but very definitely the direct cause of a large number of books.

The voyage of the *Beagle* during 1831–6 was just one in a whole succession of expeditions of all kinds: some famous, such as those of Captain Cook, whose companions included Joseph Banks, later to become President of the Royal Society, and Daniel Solander, a disciple of Linnaeus, and many more expeditions less well known. From the zoological and botanical viewpoint these voyages had their roots in Linnaeus' revolutionary system of classification, which encouraged so many naturalists to travel and discover for themselves. The main motivation, however, was usually military or political – to reconnoitre potential naval bases, for instance, to establish trading links, or just to colonize new territories – and the naturalists and artists went along as an ancillary part of the expedition.

The purpose of the *Beagle*'s voyage was to complete a survey of the South American coastline begun a few years before, and Darwin, just down from Cambridge and considered to be 'amply qualified for collating, observing and noting, anything worthy to be noted in natural history', was offered the job of naturalist accompanying the expedition. Much of his time at university had been taken up with natural history: 'No pursuit at Cambridge', he wrote, 'was followed with nearly so much eagerness or gave me so much pleasure as collecting beetles.'

Darwin's theories of the origins of living species, though they were the monumental outcome of his voyage, do not really concern us here. Although *The Origin of Species* has become the more famous book, it is *The Zoology of the Voyage of HMS Beagle* that is of more interest to us. From the point of view of its coloured plates it is not a particularly good book, but it is an interesting one, and it is worth looking at the *Beagle*'s voyage, and particularly Darwin's part in it, since it gives the lover of old natural history books some idea of how these expeditions were conducted, and the problems that had to be overcome. The *Beagle* was a type of vessel called by the sailors 'coffins', because bad weather frequently caused them to capsize and sink. The arrival of a naturalist and artist on an already small ship would have made conditions even more cramped. Darwin's ever-growing collection spread everywhere – 'I have just room to turn round, and that is all,' he wrote – and earned him the sobriquet of 'Fly-Catcher'. The ship's officers

OPPOSITE Polar Bear, Plate 41 from Audubon and Bachman's
The Quadrupeds of North America, New York, 1849–54.
This hand-coloured lithograph is from a drawing by
Audubon's son, John Woodhouse Audubon.

VENDACE.

Reithrodon Chinchilloides

were naval men with a job to do, and had a limited interest, if that, in Darwin's work. His activities both irritated and amused them; Fitzroy, the ship's captain, wrote of 'our smiles at the apparent rubbish he brought on board'. This 'rubbish', as is now well known, included a number of completely new species. One of these new species nearly escaped Darwin's notice altogether – the *Rhea Darwinii*, as he named it, was a new and rare South American emu, one of which was shot and eaten by the expedition's artist, Conrad Martens, who was unaware of its importance! Undaunted, Darwin reconstituted it from the remains.

ABOVE Lithograph of *Reithrodon Chinchilloides*, a small
mammal found on the shores of the Strait of Magellan, from
The Zoology of the Voyage of HMS Beagle.
The original drawing was by G.R. Waterhouse.

PAGES 174–5 Coloured lithograph of Grayling from
William Houghton's *British Freshwater Fishes*, London, 1879.

INSECTS

INSECTS CERTAINLY MERIT a chapter of their own, for some of the insect plates are very beautiful indeed, but it is not an easy proposition. The problem, as explained in the chapter on flowers and fruit, is that so many of the best insect plates are to be found in flower books. In spite of the title of Maria Sybilla Merian's great book *Insects of Surinam*, of 1705, it is always considered a flower book, and it would be wrong to place it anywhere else than among flower books. But it is worthwhile reminding the reader that it was Merian who discovered the metamorphosis of insects, and that a very fine plate from the *Insects of Surinam* is illustrated in colour on page 41. The plates in Mrs Bury's *Hexandrian Plants* of 1831–4 also contain some very beautiful butterflies, although she mixes plants and insects quite indiscriminately in relation to their country – or even continent – of origin. But to those of us who appreciate these books for their aesthetic appearance rather than for their zoological or botanical accuracy, this does not detract from the plates in the slightest. A plate from *Hexandrian Plants* is illustrated in colour on page 69.

Apart from these two obvious instances, examination of many other flower plates will reveal a wealth of insect life. The Prévost plates, for instance, on pages 44 and 45 contain tiny flies and snails, as do many of Ehret's, including, not surprisingly, the one from *Plantae et Papiliones Rariores* on page 20. But they are intended as mere embellishments, and we could not possibly consider these books as anything like hard-core insect books. Most of this latter category were intended to depict species from a scientific point of view, and are often accompanied by text describing the appearance, habits, life cycle, food and habitat of the insects. But insects – even spiders and beetles – are basically attractive things when illustrated, and nearly all of these 'scientific' books are also pretty.

A good-looking German book on insects is the *Insectenbelustigung* of Augustin Roesel von Rosenhof – author of the *Historia Naturalis Ranarum* illustrated in the previous chapter. The *Insectenbelustigung* was published in Nuremberg between 1740 and about 1759. Most of the plates are of groups of insects, and there are some very lovely title pages, one of which, the title page to Part II, dated 1749, is illustrated in colour on page 181.

J.J. Ernst's *Insectes d'Europe* of 1779–93 is a large quarto in eight volumes. It contains two hand-coloured frontispieces – of which that to Vol. 1 is shown in colour on page 182 – and 350 magnificently hand-coloured plates from drawings by Jacques Engramelle (by whose name, incidentally, the book is sometimes known). Only 20 copies were subscribed, which makes it a rare book indeed.

A number of good English books on insects were produced in the eighteenth century. Benjamin Wilkes' *Twelve New Designs of British Butterflies* is a folio of 1742. Wilkes was both artist and author, and his book was published by 'B. Wilkes against the Horn Tavern in Fleet Street. Where any gentleman or lady may see his collection of insects.' The first edition, from which the plate illustrated in colour on page 186 is taken, is very rare. It contains a hand-coloured dedication and 12 hand-coloured groups of butterflies. Not everyone likes to see butterflies arranged in this rather regimented way, but it is an effective way of showing a number of different butterflies together, as here, and to me it is a very charming plate. Wilkes produced a number of other insect books, perhaps the best known of which is *The English Moths and Butterflies* of *c.* 1749.

Moses Harris' *The Aurelian* of 1758–66 is almost as much a flower book as an insect book, and a very fine example of both. One of the plates, bearing a characteristic dedication – in this case to 'the Revd Mr Willm Ray' – is illustrated in colour on page 183. Among Harris' other books, which were clearly intended to be at least as instructive as they were beautiful, were *The English Lepidoptera; Or, the Aurelian's Pocket Companion*, an octavo, as one might expect from such a title, published in 1775; *An Essay Precedeing a Supplement to the Aurelian: Wherein Are Considered the Tendons and Membranes of the Wings of Butterflies; First as Useful in Describing the Situation of Their Spots or Markings; Secondly of Great Assistance in Discovering Their Different Genera . . .*, 1767–80, with eight copper engravings; and *An Exposition of English Insects, with Curious Observations and Remarks, Wherein Each Insect is Particularly Described*, 1776–80, with 50 engravings.

Dru Drury's *Illustrations of Natural History* of 1770–82 is a three-volume quarto containing 50 plates. As the typically effusive full title tells us, the book is one 'Wherein Are Exhibited Upwards of Two Hundred and Forty Figures of Exotic Insects, According to Their Different Genera'. The plate illustrated in colour on page 184 is Plate 49, un-named, from Vol. 1. Drury's accompanying informative notes tell us something about this butterfly and its provenance:

It came from Sierra Leon in Africa, and was lent me by a gentleman who lived there some years, to take a drawing from; by whom I was informed, that 'they appear about the end of June, and soon afterwards retire among the branches of the palm-trees, where they reside till the violent rains compel them to quit that situation and live among the plants, &c. on the ground.'

Butterflies, of course, would have been relatively easy for explorers and people living in tropical countries to capture, kill and preserve; they require no specialist skinning and stuffing, and can be kept in quite a small space. The colours fade, of course, as with any dead creature, but not to such an extent that they become useless to the artist.

In his rather didactic Preface Drury tries hard to project a better image for insects:

Insects may, with great truth, be considered as a rank of beings so wonderful and extraordinary, as to strike with astonishment every observer, if we regard either their structure, powers, or use . . . . Nor are they to be considered in that contemptible light in which the generality of mankind are apt to place them. We are too prone to think every thing noxious and unnecessary if we are not fully acquainted with its uses . . . .

He goes on at some length to talk about the as yet untried potential of many insects in such areas as medicine and textile dyeing.

Edward Donovan's *Insects of India* (its full title is *An Epitome of the Natural History of the Insects of India, and the Islands in the Indian Seas*) of 1800–4 is the latest book illustrated here. Donovan, of course, did not restrict himself to insects and is well known also for books on birds and fish. *Insects of India* was by no means his only book on insects – it is in fact the second part of his *General Illustration of Entomology*, the first part being *An Epitome of the Insects of China*. The *Insects of India*, a quarto, has more than 250 plates, 58 of which are coloured, and was sponsored by the famous naturalist Sir Joseph Banks. The magnificent plate illustrated in colour on page 185 is *Papilio Ulysses*; 'Our specimens', wrote Donovan, 'are from one of the Dutch spice islands in the East Indies.' Donovan was particularly fond of using bright colours in his plates, and this is a good example.

In his Advertisement (we would call it a Foreword) Donovan defined the scope of the *Insects of India* as being 'not entirely confined to those insects found in such parts of India as are in the British possession . . . since it embraces, on the contrary, the most choice selection possible of those which inhabit every other part of that vast continent, and also the islands situated in the Indian seas'.

Of other works on insects, not illustrated here, a number are worth mentioning. Thomas Martyn, whose book on shells, *The Universal Conchologist*, is illustrated in the following chapter, also produced a number of interesting works on insects. *Aranei or a Natural History of Spiders* was published in 1793. A quarto in two parts, with either 11 or 17 copper engravings, it included 'the principal parts of the well known work on English spiders by Eleazer Albin', whose *A Natural History of Birds* is illustrated in that chapter. This was not Albin's only contribution to the literature of insects. Apart from the work mentioned (*A Natural History of Spiders, and Other Curious Insects; Illustrated with Fifty Three Copper-Plates, Engraven by the Best Hands*, of 1736), he produced in 1720 *A Natural History of English Insects*, containing 100 coloured copper engravings, which were, like those in the Birds, '. . . Curiously Engraven from the Life, and Exactly Coloured by the Author'. The plates bear dedications to various patrons. Of Martyn's other two books on insects, *The*

English Entomologist of 1792 and *Psyche, Figures of Non Descript Lepidopterous Insects . . . ,* 1797, *Psyche* is by far the most interesting to the bibliophile, for it was privately produced by Martyn and only ten or so sets of its 32 stipple engravings are known to have been printed. It is therefore incredibly rare.

American insects were well represented in the nineteenth century by James Say's *American Entomology, or Descriptions of the Insects of North America,* an octavo with 54 engravings, published in Philadelphia between 1824 and 1828. A later edition produced in 1859 contained 55 plates, 36 of which were from the original edition. These plates, however, were lithographs, the work of Bowen & Co. of Philadelphia, the lithographers of Audubon and Bachman's *The Quadrupeds of North America.* Among the artists were C.A. Le Sueur and Titian Ramsay Peale. Exotic insects, like birds, responded relatively well to the techniques of lithography and, later, chromolithography. While any attempt to depict their grace of movement was frustrated, justice was certainly done to their brilliance of colouring.

OPPOSITE Hand-coloured engraved title page
to Part II of Roesel von Rosenhof's *Insectenbelustigung,*
Nuremberg, 1740–*c.* 1759.

PAGE 182 One of the hand-coloured engraved title pages, from
a drawing by Jacques Engramelle, to J.J. Ernst's
Insectes d'Europe, Peints d'après Nature, Paris, 1779–93.

PAGE 183 Plate 36, a hand-coloured engraving with a dedication
at the foot, from Moses Harris' *The Aurelian,* London, 1758–66.

PAGE 184 Plate 49, a hand-coloured engraving from Vol. 1 of
Dru Drury's *Illustrations of Natural History,* London, 1770–82.

PAGE 185 Hand-coloured engraving of a typically exotic
butterfly, Plate 21, *Papilio Ulysses,* from Edward Donovan's
Insects of India, London, 1800–4.

PAGE 186 Plate 1, the Great Egger-Moth with various other
butterflies and moths, from Benjamin Wilkes'
Twelve New Designs of British Butterflies, London, 1742.
The hand-coloured engravings were from drawing by Wilkes,
who also wrote the text.

DER

INSECTEN=

BELUSTIGUNG

Zweyter Theil.

Ioh. Rösel fec. et exc.

INSECTES
D'EUROPE,
PEINTS D'APRES NATURE PAR M. ERNST.
Gravée
et Coloriés sous sa direction;
PREMIERE PARTIE,
LES CHENILLES CRISALIDES
et Papillons de Jour.
Decrits par le R. P. Engramelle Relig. Aug.tin Q.S.G.

SE VEND A PARIS,

Chez {
Ernst, Auteur, Rue de la Harpe, ancien College de Narbonne;
De Laguette Imprimeur-Libraire, Rue de la Vieille Draperie;
Bazan et Poignant M.d d'Estampes, Rue et hotel Serpente.
}

AVEC PRIVILEGE DU ROI.

Le Sueur pinxit.   A.J. Juillet Sculp.

To the Rev.ᵈ Mʳ Willᵐ Ray

is Plate is humbly Dedicated   by his most humble Obliged Servᵗ

HONO VINCE MALUS

Moses Harris

1. *Squarrosus*

Papilio Ulysses.

London, Published as the Act directs by E. Donovan, Feb 1st 1800.

1. *The Great Egger Moth. The Caterpillar feeds on White Thorn, goes into Chrysalis about the End of May, the*
Moth comes forth in June. 2. The Small Clouded Yellow Moth. This Fly is taken by beating the Hedges in the Month
of June. 3. The Heath-Moth. Taken in the Fly State the middle of May, in Hanging-Wood 4. The Peacock
Butterfly. The Caterpillar feeds on Nettles, goes into Chrysalis in June, the Fly appears in July. 5. The
Speckled Yellow Moth. Taken in the Fly State the beginning of May. 6. The Small Tyger Moth. The Caterpillar
feeds on Lettice, Chickweed &c. Spins up and is taken in the Fly State in May. 7. The White Admirable But-
terfly. See this Fly described in Plate 2. the 8.th No 1.

Setts Plain (or Colour'd from the Real Flyes) Printed for John Bowles at the Black Horse in Cornhill.

Published by Benjn. Wilkes, Feb y the 1. 1741. According to Act of Parliament.

Design'd by B. Wilkes.   Engrav'd by H. Roberts

1st Plate

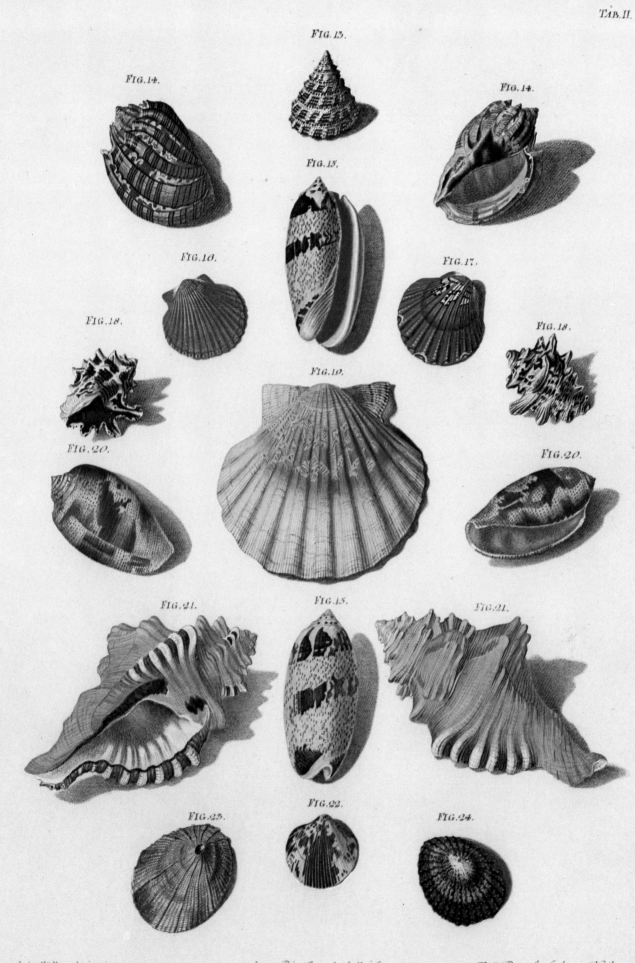

TAB.II.

FIG.13.

FIG.14.

FIG.14.

FIG.15.

FIG.16.

FIG.17.

FIG.18.

FIG.18.

FIG.19.

FIG.20.

FIG.20.

FIG.21.

FIG.13.

FIG.21.

FIG.23.

FIG.22.

FIG.24.

Gab. Müller ad viv. pinx.   Cum Priv. Sac. Caef. Majeft.   F. M. Regenfus fculp. exc. Nörib.

Collection
des differentes espèces de
COQUILLAGES
qu'on trouve dans les Mers
rassemblée
&
communiquée au Public
par
George Wolfgang Knorr
à Nuremberg.

IIde Partie

SHELLS

'THE STUDY OF SHELLS', wrote George Perry in his *Conchology* of 1811, 'or testaceous animals, is a branch of natural history which, although not greatly useful to the mechanical arts, by the beauty of the subjects it comprises, most admirably adapted to recreate the senses, to improve the taste or invention of the Artist, and, finally and insensibly to lead to the contemplation of the great excellence and wisdom of the Divinity in their formation.'

Shell-collecting became a kind of expensive hobby – sometimes an obsession – among wealthy aristocrats and scientists (including Linnaeus) in the seventeenth and eighteenth centuries, much as people today, if they can afford to do so, might collect rare stamps or Georgian silver. The difference was that in those times shells were a novelty, quite apart from their beauty, and there was the added excitement that someone had probably risked his life diving among coral reefs to find them. The competition for new and rare shells was fierce – not unnaturally, a number of frauds were perpetrated by the unscrupulous – and some of the collections became as famous as Seba's cabinet of curiosities which he drew on for his *Thesaurus*. Seba, incidentally, included shells among his curiosities, but arranged them in pretty patterns, as one might piece together a mosaic, rather than in any zoological scheme. Many of these collections of shells became the material for shell books.

Shells represent possibly the least important area of natural history books from the collector's point of view, and the plates vary from extraordinarily dull to very pretty indeed. In view of these latter very good shell plates, shells receive rather more attention here than perhaps they deserve. Most shell books were intended as an aid to identification, though the shells were often arranged quite haphazardly in the plates, and the books were not what one might call well-organized guides.

Franz Michael Regenfuss' *Auserlesne Schnecken* of 1758 is a typical example. It is among the earliest books on shells and shellfish, and Linnaeus' system had not yet been

OPPOSITE Hand-coloured engraved title page to Part II of
Georg Wolfgang Knorr's *Collection Générale des Différentes
Espèces des Coquillages*, Nuremberg, 1760–73.

PAGE 187 Plate 2, a hand-coloured engraving, from
Franz Michael Regenfuss' *Auserlesne Schnecken*, Copenhagen, 1758.
Regenfuss' patron was the King of Denmark and Norway,
whose name appears below the plate.

applied to shells. The book was published in two large folio volumes in Copenhagen. The text was in both French and German, and the book is often known by its French title, *Choix de Coquillages et de Crustacés*. It has the largest format of any shell book ever produced, and the 24 superb plates, one of which is shown in colour on page 187, were drawn mostly by Regenfuss himself, and coloured by his wife. The shells were not, however, rare or unknown ones at that time – frankly, Regenfuss drew whatever was offered to him, but he drew them extremely well and the book is a good one from that standpoint. The book's place of publication is explained by the fact that, after a rather unsatisfactory start, Regenfuss was sponsored by the King of Denmark and Norway, who made him his court engraver.

Another highly attractive work is the German engraver Georg Wolfgang Knorr's *Collection des Différentes Espèces des Coquillages*, published in six quarto volumes in Nuremberg between 1760 and 1773. It contains six hand-coloured engraved title pages – that for Part II is illustrated in colour on page 188 – and 190 plates. The book has a complicated history: there are various editions in a number of languages and the plates do not always tally. All the plates, with the exception of a few uncoloured ones done after Knorr's death, are very well drawn and painted, but again, as in Regenfuss' book, they are in no comprehensible order.

Thomas Martyn's *The Universal Conchologist* is probably the greatest of all books on shells. Published in four folio volumes between 1784 and 1787, it has 160 hand-coloured plates. For once this is a book in which the author has tried to impose some order on his shells – its full title is *The Universal Conchologist, Exhibiting the Figure of Every Known Shell Accurately Drawn and Painted after Nature: A New Systematic Arrangement By the Author.*

ABOVE Plate 30, a hand-coloured engraving from
Thomas Martyn's *The Universal Conchologist*, London, 1784–7.

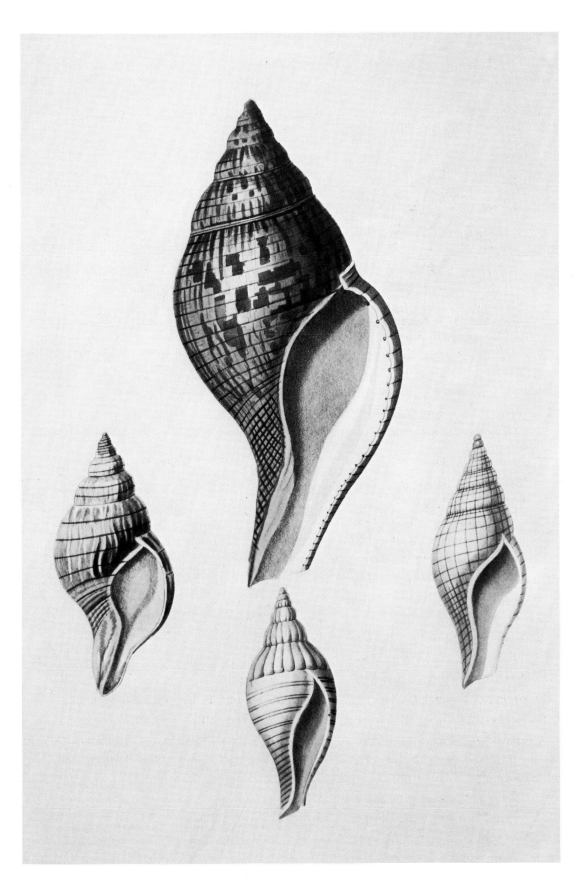

Hand-coloured engraving of *Pyrula*, Plate 30 from
George Perry's *Conchology*, London, 1811.

In his Introduction Martyn discusses the variety and beauty of shells, and points out that, though many prized collections have been assembled, no one has yet (in his opinion) done them justice in a book:

In the various figures of Shells the hand of the supreme Artist has displayed every gradation of beauty which can exist in permanent form. From the most rude and mishapen oyster, scarcely to be distinguished from its native rock, the scale regularly ascends till it arrives at perfection in the superior symmetry of the *Spiral Snail* . . . .

The variety of species of Shells is immense, and their curious marks and variegated colours are no less objects of our astonishment and delight. Accordingly, many great Princes, as well as other illustrious and learned persons, in all ages, have spared no expense to form superb collections of these elegant subjects . . . .

The Universal Conchologist, like Knorr's book, varies, but in this case from copy to copy. Some have gold embellishments, some have frames around the plates, some are well drawn and carefully etched, while others look flat and two-dimensional – all within the same copy. The shells illustrated were bought by Martyn in 1780 specifically for this book, and represent the whole collection acquired during Captain Cook's third voyage to the South Seas. Martyn had a studio of young artists, which he ran on *quasi-monastic* lines, to provide the illustrations for the copper engravings in his books. The assumption was that, schooled solely by him in all matters, including particularly religion and art, they would all produce very similar work.

The last shell book to be discussed here is of a rather different nature from the others. George Perry's *Conchology*, a folio with 61 hand-coloured plates, published in 1811, is in a way the most enjoyable of shell books. Its plates are somewhat idiosyncratic pictures of shells in weird and improbable colours, with peculiar-sounding names. They later caused some derision in natural history circles, particularly from James Sowerby, whose own book, *The Genera of Recent and Fossil Shells*, was a direct competitor. One critic wrote of Perry's 'absurd names and pantomimic display of figures'. John Gray – author of *Gleanings from the Menagerie and Aviary at Knowsley Hall* – then a young man working at the British Museum, was innocent enough to quote Perry as an authority for a certain problem of nomenclature, and was ridiculed for it. But time has vindicated both Gray and Perry; *Conchology* has been reinstated as a serious shell book and some of Perry's 'absurd' names are now the commonly accepted ones.

Printing Techniques

NATURAL HISTORY PLATES have been made by a variety of techniques through the centuries, and it is not possible to appreciate their finer points without knowing something of the methods involved and the results that could be achieved. The great age of natural history books can be divided into three periods:

Its Rise, 1700–80 The first books with coloured illustrations began to be produced about 1700. Copper engraving, hand-coloured, was the medium of illustration.

The Grand Era, 1780–1830 The copper engravings continued, but the most important works were illustrated with stipple engravings in France, and with aquatint or mezzotint in Britain. The plates of this period were partly printed in colours, partly coloured by hand.

The Gradual Decline, 1830–60 and later This was the age of the lithograph, originally an interesting method with hand-coloured plates, but one that became ever cheaper, and finally, after the arrival of chromolithography, sometimes very nasty indeed.

TECHNIQUES BEFORE 1700

The wood-cut, first developed around 1400, was the earliest method of all. It had ceased to be used on a large scale by 1700, when our period starts, but it is perhaps worth a mention to point out the basic principles of printing.

The original picture was first copied on to a wood block. Then the space between the drawn lines was cut away with a sharp knife, so that these lines, standing proud of the rest of the block, would receive the ink and in due course print black. The image had to be drawn and carved in reverse, of course, as with all the methods of printing discussed here, so that when the inked block was pressed on to a sheet of paper the print made by it would be the right way round. (Sometimes engravers and printers forgot to do this – the George Edwards plate on page 83, for instance, bears script and numbers, some of which are the right way round, while others are reversed!)

Wood engraving is a refinement of the wood-cut, in which the engraver uses a burin, the fine steel cutting tool of copper engravers, to obtain a multitude of fine lines that result in subtle gradations of grey tones.

COPPER ENGRAVING

This method was used throughout the eighteenth century and into the early nineteenth, and a large number of very fine plates were produced in this way. The original drawing was transferred on to a copper plate in reverse, usually by tracing or similar means. Then the lines were cut away with a burin – the deeper the cut, the more ink it takes up and the blacker is the eventual printed line. The plate was then inked and the print was taken from it.

Copper engraving, like the wood-cut and wood engraving, was basically a lineal method and did not allow for very much in the way of light and shade. The following methods enabled more sophisticated effects to be achieved.

MEZZOTINT

The mezzotint was invented in Germany in the seventeenth century. To prepare a copper plate for mezzotint printing it was first roughened all over its surface so that it would, if left like this, print completely black. Then the engraver proceeded to reduce the intensity of the blackness where he wanted lighter areas to appear, by scraping off the roughness with a tool called a rocker. He worked from dark to light, rather than from light to dark, as in the preceding methods. The rocker blade consisted of a number of tiny teeth which made zigzag marks on the plates. It was a laborious task, as the rocker had to be used many times in every direction. When the plate was considered to have been rocked sufficiently, the design was transferred on to it, in reverse, with a scraper.

With this method, as with the aquatint described below, the plates wore each time a print was taken from them, so that no two prints were ever exactly the same. Often the plate needed retouching, which made a further difference to the next print, and on occasion the whole plate had to be re-modelled. The best example of this is *The Temple of Flora*.

Mezzotint plates were often colour-printed, since surface printing methods like this were better suited to colour printing than were line processes. Colour printing itself is described below.

STIPPLE ENGRAVING

This was an etching rather than an engraving technique – in other words acid, rather than a tool, was used to cut into the copper plate. The plate was first covered with a substance such as varnish, which was impervious to acid. Using etching needles and punches the design was then copied over in the form of small dots which penetrated this etching ground and went right through to the copper beneath. The dots were larger and close together where the design was to be the darkest, and small and far apart where a light effect was required. When the acid was applied it ate through the copper in which the dots had been punched – more or less deeply, according to the size of dot – leaving intact only the parts covered with the ground. Very fine details were sometimes added by retouching the plate afterwards. A very delicate and varied tone was produced, which was generally used with colour printing on the plate, if necessary retouched by hand later.

Stipple engraving was the method used for the plates of the great French masters Redouté, Bessa and Prévost in the late eighteenth and early nineteenth centuries. Bartolozzi invented the method in England, but it came to full flower in France, and Langlois was perhaps the greatest French engraver.

AQUATINT

The main difference between the aquatint and the stipple engraving was that in the aquatint the etching ground was porous. Acid was applied to the plate many times; as soon as a particular area was sufficiently bitten into, it was covered with a non-porous ground, and so on until the darkest areas had been dealt with. Any area that was to print pure white was completely covered with the non-porous ground to start with. This method produced a kind of soft half-tone effect. As with mezzotints, the plates wore and had to be continually worked on, so apparently identical prints produced by this method may contain a number of minor differences.

SOFT GROUND ETCHING

Soft ground etching was the method used for the plates of John Edwards' *A Collection of Flowers Drawn After Nature*, and for no other natural history book. These plates, which appeared between 1783 and 1801, used 'light' only for the etched tints, and it is possible to think that one is looking at a pure watercolour.

In this method the etching ground was mixed with tallow, and was therefore softer. The design was drawn or traced on a sheet of paper laid over the ground, and the softness of the ground enabled the etcher to cut the lines through it on to the plate beneath. Acid was then applied, and worked in the same way as with stipple engraving.

COLOUR PRINTING

Some natural history plates were entirely colour-printed, while others, including the great works of Thornton, Redouté and Levaillant, were partially colour-printed and retouched by hand afterwards. There were two ways of colour printing from the plate – applying all the colours on to a single copper plate (the method favoured in England), or making several identical copper plates, applying a different colour to each, and printing them on to the paper one after another. This latter method was the one used in France.

LITHOGRAPHY

The technique of lithography was invented accidentally by an Austrian, Alois Senefelder, in 1796. In a hurry one day, he wrote down his mother's laundry list on a handy stone – he had been conducting etching experiments using various objects as 'plates' – and when he later tried to wash off the writing with acid and water he found he could not, since the ink was greasy. By about 1840 lithography had ousted all other techniques.

In the perfected method a smooth lithographic stone received the design in pen and greasy ink or a greasy lithographic crayon. The softness of the crayon gave a rather imprecise line, and lithographic plates were frequently improved by retouching with a scraper or by various other methods. The stone was then wetted, but the inked parts rejected the moisture. When a greasy ink was passed over the stone, however, it was accepted by the previously inked portions. The lithograph was frequently hand-coloured, which accounts for its superiority to the chromolithograph.

Apart from the difference in appearance, a lithographic print does not have the plate mark which surrounds engravings, so is easily distinguishable.

CHROMOLITHOGRAPHY

This is the name given to colour printing using lithographic methods. The plates could be printed many times over, with blocks of colour overlapping and overprinting to create a range of colours. As many lithographic stones were needed as there were colours to be applied. This multiple printing gave the plates a rather greasy, shiny appearance, suitable for the vivid plumage of tropical birds but much less so for flower prints. The process required considerable skill to do it well, because of the multiple printing. This explains why, especially late in the period, so many bad chromolithographic plates were produced.

Natural history plates frequently carry a number of credits to the various people involved in preparing them. Since Latin abbreviations are usually used they can be perplexing to the uninitiated. Below is a brief glossary of these terms.

Del.: stands for *delineavit* or *delineaverunt* – Latin for he (or she) or they drew – and therefore refers to the artist. This is usually found on the bottom left-hand side of the print, after the artist's name.

Dir.: stands for *direxit* or *direxerunt*, and refers to the person(s) who supervised the engraving (i.e. not necessarily the actual engraver). The name precedes it.

Exc.: stands for *excudit* or *excuderunt*, meaning (it always follows a name) engraved by, or sometimes engraved and printed.

Fe. or *Fec.*: stands for *fecit* or *fecerunt*, meaning made by. A less common variant of *del*. The name always precedes it.

Imp.: stands for *impressit* or *impresserunt*, meaning printed by. On French plates it often stands for *imprimé* or *Imprimerie* – it all means the same thing. This information is usually found below the title of the plate.

Lith. or *Lit.*: refers to the lithographer, whose name it follows.

Pinx.: stands for *pinxit* or *pinxerunt*, meaning painted by. In this context it is a less common alternative to *del*. *Pinx.* also sometimes denotes the hand-colourist.

Sc. or *Sculp.*: stands for *sculpsit* or *sculpserunt*, meaning engraved by. It follows the engraver's name and is usually found on the bottom right-hand side of a plate.

BOOK SIZES

The general reader – and the expert will have no need to read this account anyway – wants to know within reason how large a book is, and not to be told this in too technical a way. When a sheet of paper from the printers has been folded once it is called a folio, and produces two leaves, that is four numbered pages. Folded again it is a quarto – four leaves, eight pages. A large number of ordinary books are octavo, with eight leaves and therefore sixteen pages from each original printer's sheet. Smaller books can be 12mo, 16mo, 24mo and 32mo.

The American Century Dictionary gives 30 different sizes of folio, quarto and octavo books. Most readers do not want to know all these details, and do not mind how many times a sheet has been folded. So I have always borne this in mind and written about 'large folio', 'folio', 'small folio', and so on. One problem is that the terms are not used consistently; to me, for instance, a large quarto is a folio, and I call it this! A small quarto is sometimes called an octavo. Quarto books are, however, almost always square or squarish, while folios and octavos are taller than they are wide.

There is one exception to all this – very, very large books, such as Audubon's *The Birds of America*, or the somewhat smaller Thornton's *The Temple of Flora*, must be distinguished somehow, so to me the first is elephant folio (some prefer double elephant folio), and the latter is very large folio. Remember also that most large natural history books came out either in parts, or in their original boards, and the most valuable ones were bound more proudly by their owners afterwards, some in full calf binding, some in half calf, and some in full or half morocco. The best of these bindings are contemporary, but some, less fortunately – for their value at any rate – are modern. In all cases, or very nearly all, this made the original size smaller. If we want to be really fussy, or perhaps it is better to say really accurate, we must give the size of books in inches and centimetres, both in height and breadth. However, since the original sheets from the printers varied in size, this would have to be done for every single book. As an approximate guide we can think of elephant, the largest size encountered, as about 30×40 inches (Audubon's *Birds* is actually $29\frac{1}{2} \times 39\frac{1}{2}$), with folio, quarto and so on correspondingly smaller.

WATERMARKS

Good, hand-made paper such as was used for natural history plates always contained a watermark, made by pressing a wire shape against the paper during the making process. The watermark consisted of the paper-maker's name and usually the date, and was invisible unless held up against the light, when it could, and still can, be seen with a little difficulty. The date is particularly important with mezzotints and aquatints, since every time a print was pressed on to and then pulled off the plate, the plate wore, as described above, so that in fact no two prints were exactly the same.

If a print is dated 1806 and the watermark is dated, say, 1818, the print cannot have been a very early issue. If the watermark says 1802, the chances are high that it will be one of the earliest issues. Anyone with a real interest in the subject should look very carefully at watermarks.

It is perhaps a fair moment to add a little story. Just after the Second World War, I was alone in the book sale-room at Sotheby's, looking at a copy of *The Temple of Flora*. The only way to examine the watermark was to lie flat on the floor and hold the book on a chair with the print that I wanted to see separated, and with the light behind it. This was not easy, and took all my attention.

By degrees I became aware of a tap-tapping noise near me and, looking up, saw first a parasol and then Queen Mary holding it. In utter confusion, I tried respectfully to get up, but was waved firmly back into position by the Queen, who said, 'Good evening,' and passed on. Queen Mary knew a great deal about many kinds of antiques, and I feel sure that her sympathies were with me.

Appendix

A 1934 Catalogue

THIS IS A REPRINT, with one or two slight amendments, of a catalogue of flower and bird books which I compiled in the 1930s when I was involved in running an antiquarian bookshop. I have talked about prices, and about the amazing number of very fine books which were included in this catalogue, in the Introduction, so I will say no more now and let the catalogue speak for itself.

CATALOGUE No. 6

from

THREE CURZON STREET, MAYFAIR, LONDON, W. I

OLD COLOUR PLATE BOOKS OF FLOWERS AND BIRDS

from 1730 onwards, including a number of French works with the plates printed in colours from the drawings of P. J. Redouté; a complete set of Robert Sweet's *British Flower Garden*, 7 volumes, and of his *Florist's Guide*, 2 volumes; and a collection of books on American ornithology.

A Collection of French Flower Books
1783 – 1845

including a number with the plates printed in colours.

1 BUCHOZ, M. § LE JARDIN D'EDEN.   Le Paradis Terrestre renouvellé dans le jardin de la Reine à Trianon.   *Folio, half calf.* Paris 1783.   With 200 coloured plates of flowers and plants. Rare.   £30

2 VENTENAT, E. P. § JARDIN DE LA MALMAISON.   1803. Original parts with wrappers bound in.   Entirely uncut.   *Folio, bound in old sheep.*   A superb copy with the 120 plates by P. J. REDOUTÉ, printed in colours, in spotless condition.   Very rare.   £70

3 PREVOST, JEAN-LOUIS. § COLLECTION DES FLEURS ET DES FRUITS PEINTS D'APRES NATURE.   *Large folio, half pigskin.*   Rather rubbed.   Paris 1805.   With 48 exquisite groups of flowers printed in colours.   One of the most perfect specimens of French colour printing of this period, and with the flowers charmingly arranged in bouquets.   Title page repaired, and bottom corners of pages slightly dogged, but the plates are spotless.   Very rare.   £100

4 BONPLAND, A. § DESCRIPTION DES PLANTES RARES CULTIVÉES À MALMAISON ET À NAVARRE.   *Large folio, half morocco, red roan cloth.*   A fine copy.   Paris 1813.   With 64 plates drawn by REDOUTÉ and printed in colours. A superb book, the rarest of all works illustrated by Redouté.   A mint copy of the large paper edition.   £60

5 PALISOT DE BEAUVOIS, BARON. § FLORE D'OWARE ET DE BENIN EN AFRIQUE.   Two volumes.   *Folio, half red morocco, roan cloth, gilt.*   A fine copy.   With 120 coloured plates.   An extremely rare book of which not more than 20 copies were printed.   Paris 1804.   £75

6 PLANSON, J. A. § ICONOGRAPHIE DU GENRE OEILLET OU CHOIX DES OEILLETS LES PLUS BEAUX ET LES PLUS RARES. *Folio, half morocco.* Paris 1845. With 200 varieties of carnations on 50 coloured plates. A few spots on several plates but the plates as a whole in fine state. A delightful and rare book. £25

7 DUHAMEL DU MONCEAU. § TRAITE DES ARBRES ET ARBUSTES QUE L'ON CULTIVE EN PLEINE TERRE EN EUROPE ET PARTICULIEREMENT EN FRANCE. Edition augmentée de plus de moitié pour le nombre des espèces. Redige par Mm. Veillard &c. 7 volumes. *Folio, marbled boards.* A fine copy, 1825. With 500 magnificent coloured plates by REDOUTÉ and BESSA. One of the finest of all French coloured books of this period, the plates are beautifully printed in colours and are in fine state. £50

8 —NOUVEAU TRAITE DES ARBRES FRUITIERS. Nouvelle édition augmentée de plus moitié par Mm. Veillard &c. 2 volumes. *Large folio, marbled boards.* A superb copy of the large paper edition with 145 coloured plates on vellum paper. The plates again are by REDOUTÉ and BESSA. N.D. (1810). £20

9 RISSO, A. & POITEAU, A. § HISTOIRE NATURELLE DES ORANGERS. *Folio, half green morocco, gilt.* A very fine binding. Essex House copy with coronet and monogram: 'sx' tooled on back. Paris 1818. With 109 plates printed in colours. £28

10 POITEAU, A. § POMOLOGIE FRANCAISE. Recueil des plus beaux fruits cultivés en France. 4 Volumes. *Folio, half tree calf, gilt.* Paris 1846. With 429 (of 433) magnificent coloured plates of fruit. A few leaves damaged slightly by offset from the plates but a very fine copy of one of the rarest books on fruit. £65

11 SERTUM BOTANICUM: COLLECTION DE PLANTES REMARQUABLES PAR LEUR UTILITÉ, LEUR ÉLÉGANCE, LEUR ÉCLAT OU LEUR NOUVEAUTÉ. Par une société de Botanistes. 16 volumes. *Folio, original boards.* 1829–30. With 600 coloured plates of flowers. An important and splendidly executed book. £30

12 FLORE DE L'AMATEUR, CHOIX DES PLANTES PUBLIÉES DANS LE SERTUM BOTANICUM. 2 volumes. *Folio, half morocco.* N.D. (1830). With 200 coloured plates of flowers taken from the above-mentioned work. £12 10s

13 DRAPIEZ, M. § HERBIER DE L'AMATEUR DE FLEURS. 8 volumes. *4to, half calf, marbled boards.* Uncut. 1828–35. With 600 coloured plates of flowers, very delicately and accurately executed. A most charming and complete work. £20

14 ROQUES, J. § PHYTOGRAPHIE MEDICALE ORNÉES DE FIGURES COLORIÉES DE GRANDEUR NATURELLE OU L'ON EXPOSE L'HISTOIRE DES POISONS TIRÉS DU RÈGNE VÉGÉTAL. 2 volumes. *4to, half calf, marbled boards.* Paris 1821. With 180 delicately drawn and coloured plates. £10 10s

15 CHAUMETON, F. P. § FLORE MEDICALE. 8 volumes. *4to.* Large paper copy. *Bound in half morocco.* 1814–20. With 405 coloured plates. This edition of the book with the plates on thick paper is quite uncommon. £10 10s

16 VIGNEUX, A. § FLORE PITTORESQUE DES ENVIRONS DE PARIS. *4to. Tree calf.* 1812. With map and 62 coloured plates, showing four flowers on each plate. £4 10s

16A DENISSE, E. § FLORE D'AMERIQUE. *Folio, original 12 parts.* Paris. N.D. (1843–6). With 72 richly coloured lithographs of American flowers. No text. Rare and very decorative. £21

A few German and Dutch coloured Herbals and Flower Books

17 WEINMANN, J. H. § TAALRYK REGISTER DER PLAAT – OFTE FIGUUR – BESCHRYUINGEN DER BLOEMDRAGENDE GEWASSEN. 4 volumes. *Folio, contemporary calf, gilt.* A very fine copy. Amsterdam 1736–48. With fine mezzotint frontispiece, and 1026 superb plates of plants and flowers, printed in colours, a very early specimen of colour-printing. Rare. £42

18 KNORR, G. W. § DAS REICH DER BLUMEN, REGNUM FLORAE. *Folio. half calf.* Rubbed. Nuremberg. N.D. (1740). 200 coloured plates of flowers and plants. A very fine example of an early coloured German herbal. £27 10s

19 KNOOP, J. H. § POMOLOGIA. *Folio, tree calf, gilt.* Finely tooled. A beautiful copy. 1748 (published Leeuwarden, Holland). With 39 interesting coloured plates of fruit. A rare book. £5

20 A BEAUTIFUL DUTCH FLOWER BOOK: NEDERLANDSCH BLOEMWERK. *4to, half calf.* Amsterdam 1794. With coloured floral title page, showing a group of flowers in a vase and 53 very fine coloured plates. £15

21 REIDER, J. E. VON. § ANNALEN DER BLUMISTEREI. 8 volumes. *Post 8vo, tree calf, gilt, coloured edges.* Leipzig, 1826–32. With 192 very charming coloured plates of flowers. £8 8s

English Flower Books

22 FURBER, R. § THE FLOWER GARDEN DISPLAYED in above four hundred curious representations of the most beautiful flowers, regularly disposed in the respective months of their blossom, curiously engraved on copper plates from the designs of Mr. Furber and others and coloured to the life. *4to, full contemporary calf, gilt.* A very fine copy. 1734. With coloured floral frontispiece and twelve magnificent coloured groups of flowers arranged in vases, very decoratively.   £17 17s

23 CARWITHAM, J. § THE COMPLEAT FLORIST. *8vo, contemporary calf.* A very fine copy with coloured frontispiece and magnificent floral title page which is reproduced on the cover of this catalogue: and with 100 coloured illustrations of flowers. A rare and beautiful book. 1747.   £17 10s

24 BOWLES'S FLORIST containing 60 plates of beautiful flowers regularly disposed in their succession of blowing. *8vo, half calf.* 1777. The plates are attractively drawn and coloured. A good copy of a rare book.   £14

25 HILL, JOHN. § EDEN or a compleat body of Gardening, containing plain and familiar directions for raising the several useful products of a garden, fruits, roots and herbage, together with the culture of all kinds of flowers. *Folio, Russia gilt.* A fine copy. 1757. With coloured frontispiece of the Genius of Botany explaining to the gardener the characters of plants while Flora and Pomona offer him their choicest products. And with 60 fine coloured plates.   £14

26 —THE BRITISH HERBAL: an history of plants and trees, natives of Britain. *Folio, calf, gilt.* 1756. With coloured frontispiece representing the Genius of Health receiving the tributes of Europe, Asia, Africa and America and delivering them to the British Reader: and with 75 coloured plates showing many hundreds of plants and flowers.   £15 15s

27 ANDREWS, H. § THE BOTANIST'S REPOSITORY. Comprising coloured illustrations of new and rare plants only, with botanical descriptions in Latin and English after the Linnaean system. 6 volumes (should be 10). *4to, Russia.* Rather rubbed. With 432 fine coloured plates, one or two slightly damaged by offset, but in the main in beautiful state. 1797. A complete set of this work is exceedingly rare, and as long a run as this is quite unusual. Few botanical artists have such a reputation as Andrews, and of few are the works so eagerly sought.   £18 18s

28 —GERANIUMS. *4to, half morocco, gilt.* 1804. A fine copy with 94 (should be 124) coloured plates: a copy as near perfect as this is quite unusual, as complete copies are very rare.   £21

29 SALISBURY, R. A. & HOOKER, W. § PARADISUS LONDINENSIS containing plants cultivated in the vicinity of the Metropolis. Volume 1, parts 1 and 2 (all published). *4to, contemporary half Russia (neatly rebacked).* Entirely uncut 1806. With 113 coloured plates (should be 119). A very rare book, even imperfect copies being exceedingly difficult to find.   £15

30 HOOKER, W. § POMONA LONDINENSIS. Containing coloured engravings of the most esteemed fruits cultivated in the British gardens. Volume 1 (all published). *Small folio, calf.* Rather worn. 1818. With 49 fine coloured plates. Rare. Royal Horticultural Society's copy presented by the author in parts.   £12 10s

31 SWEET, R. § THE BRITISH FLOWER GARDEN. The complete edition in seven volumes, being the two series. *Royal 8vo, half red calf, top edge gilt.* A nice set. 1838. With 712 coloured plates. A complete set of Sweet is very difficult to obtain, and this one has all the plates in spotless condition.   £36

32 —THE BRITISH FLOWER GARDEN. Containing coloured figures and descriptions of the most ornamental and curious hardy herbacious plants including annuals, biennials and perennials. *Royal 8vo.* First series, 3 volumes; second series, 2 volumes (should be 4). In all 5 volumes. 1st series bound in *full morocco gilt;* 2nd series in *half morocco, backs uniform, all edges gilt.* A very fine set, with 500 plates. Sweet's books are perhaps, together with Andrews', the most sought after of any British botanist. 1823–33.   £22

33 —THE FLORIST'S GUIDE and cultivator's directory containing coloured figures of the choicest flowers cultivated by florists including ranunculus carnations, picotees, pinks, georginas, polyanthus, auriculas, hyacinths and tulips. 2 volumes. *Royal 8vo, original boards.* A spotless copy with 200 coloured plates. 1827–31.   £18 18s

34 —GERANIACEAE. 3 volumes (should be 5). *8vo, half calf.* 1820–6. With 300 (should be 500) coloured plates. A complete set of this book is very rare indeed and even a run like this is not often found.   £12

35 HOOKER, W. J. § EXOTIC FLORA.   Containing figures and descriptions of new, rare or otherwise interesting exotic plants.   3 volumes.   *8vo, half morocco.*   1823–7.   With 232 coloured plates.   £9 9s

36 CURTIS, W. § LECTURES ON BOTANY as delivered to his pupils, arranged by S. Curtis.   2 volumes.   *8vo, half morocco, gilt extra.*   Marbled boards and edges.   A very fine copy.   1803–4.   With portrait of Curtis and with 114 coloured plates.   £2 10s

37 EDWARDS, SYDENHAM. § THE NEW BOTANIC GARDEN, illustrated by 133 plants engraved by Sansom from the original pictures and coloured with greatest exactness.   1812.   2 volumes.   *4to, half calf.*   Entirely uncut.   With 60 coloured plates.   £6 15s

38 —Another copy.   2 volumes in 1.   *Contemporary straight-grained blue morocco.*   With 60 coloured plates.   £6

39 McDONALD, A. § COMPLETE DICTIONARY OF PRACTICAL GARDENING.   2 volumes.   *4to, half calf.*   Rather rubbed.   1807.   With 60 coloured plates of flowers from original drawings by Sydenham Edwards.   £4

40 McINTOSH, CHARLES. § FLORA AND POMONA or the British fruit and flower garden.   *4to, morocco, gilt, gilt edges.*   1829.   With 71 attractively drawn coloured plates of flowers and fruit.   Scarce.   £8 15s

41 SMITH, J. E. § EXOTIC BOTANY consisting of coloured figures and scientific descriptions of such new beautiful or rare plants as are worthy of cultivation in the gardens of Britain.   The figures by James Sowerby.   1804.   2 volumes in 1.   *4to, contemporary green straight-grained morocco, gilt, gilt edges.*   A very fine copy.   With 120 coloured plates.   £7 7s

42 BROOKSHAW, G. § POMONA BRITANNICA, or a collection of the most esteemed fruits cultivated in Great Britain.   2 volumes in 1.   *4to, calf, gilt, marbled edges.*   1817.   With 60 fine coloured aquatint plates.
                £14 14s

43 —GROUPS OF FLOWERS, FRUIT AND BIRDS drawn and accurately coloured after nature with full directions for the young artist.   *Folio, full crimson straight-grained morocco, gilt, gilt edges.*   With 18 fine coloured groups and 18 duplicate uncoloured plates.   2nd (best) edition.   1819.   £8 8s

44 —A NEW TREATISE ON FLOWER PAINTING or Every Lady her own Drawing Master. Containing Familiar and Easy Instructions for acquiring a perfect knowledge of Drawing Flowers with Accuracy and Taste and Complete Directions for producing the various Tints.   4to, original boards.   With 12 finely coloured plates, and duplicate plates, uncoloured.   1818.   £1 10s

45 ROSCOE, MRS. EDWARD. § FLORAL ILLUSTRATIONS OF THE SEASONS.   *4to, half morocco, gilt.*   With 55 coloured illustrations engraved by R. Havell Jun., of 'the most beautiful, hardy and rare Herbaceous Plants cultivated in the flower garden'.   1829.   £8 10s

45A HENDERSON, P. § THE SEASONS AND FLOWER GARDEN.   Being a selection of the most beautiful flowers that blossom at the four seasons of the year.   *4to, original boards.*   Mint copy.   Ackermann, 1806.   With coloured title page and 23 very fine coloured plates.   Rare.   £18 10s

46 THE POMOLOGICAL MAGAZINE or figures and descriptions of the most important varieties of fruit cultivated in Great Britain.   3 volumes.   *8vo, original cloth, gilt edges.*   With 152 plates of fruit, very finely coloured.   1828–30.   £7 10s

47 EVERARD, ANNE. § FLOWERS FROM NATURE, with the botanical name, class and order, and instructions for copying.   Lithographed and coloured from drawings.   *Folio, morocco, gilt.*   With 13 very fine plates.   1835.   £1 15s

48 LINDLEY, J. § ROSARUM MONOGRAPHIA or a botanical History of Roses, with nineteen coloured plates.   *Royal 8vo, original boards.*   1820.   Rare.   £3 17s 6d

49 —POMOLOGIA BRITANNICA or figures and descriptions of the most important varieties of fruit cultivated in Great Britain.   3 volumes.   *8vo, half morocco, gilt, gilt edges.*   1841.   With 152 fine coloured plates.   £6 15s

50 PAXTON.   § BOTANICAL MAGAZINE.   8 volumes.   *8vo, half morocco.*   A fine run. 1834–41.   With over 300 coloured plates.   £8 10s

51 LOUDON, MRS. § THE LADIES' FLOWER GARDEN OF ORNAMENTAL ANNUALS, PERENNIALS, GREENHOUSE PLANTS AND BULBOUS PLANTS.   4 volumes.   *4to, half morocco, gilt, gilt tops.*   2nd edition.   N.D. (1850).   A fine set with 238 coloured groups of flowers.   £16 16s

52 —THE LADIES' FLOWER GARDEN OF ORNAMENTAL ANNUALS, PERENNIAL AND BULBOUS PLANTS together with BRITISH WILD FLOWERS.   4 volumes in 5.   *4to, half morocco, gilt, gilt tops.*   A very fine set.   1843–9.   With 262 coloured groups of flowers.   £18 18s

53   We have also odd volumes of all of Mrs. Loudon's works, bound in the *original cloth* or in *half morocco*, all with the plates in fine state, 44–96 plates in each volume.   Price from £3 to £5 10s per volume.

54   BUSBY, T. L. § THE ELEMENTS OF FLOWER & FRUIT PAINTING.   Illustrated with engravings from studies after nature by Madame Vincent.   *Large 4to, half calf.*   With 23 plates in two states, printed in colours and uncoloured.   A very fine work.   £8 15s

55   SMITH, F. W. § THE FLORISTS' MUSEUM.   A register of the newest and most beautiful varieties of Florists' Flowers.   *4to, original cloth, gilt edges.*   N.D. (1835).   With coloured title page of a group of flowers and 59 fine coloured plates.   £4 4s

56   CURTIS, H. § BEAUTIES OF THE ROSE.   2 volumes.   Large paper edition.   *Folio, full crimson morocco, gilt, gilt edges.*   Fine copies.   With 38 richly coloured plates.   1850–3.   Scarce.   £10 10s

57   —Small paper edition.   2 volumes in 1.   *4to, full crimson morocco, gilt, gilt edges.*   A beautiful copy, with 38 coloured plates.   £7 10s

58   McINTOSH, C. § THE FLOWER GARDEN.   *Post 8vo, original cloth.*   1839.   Coloured title page and 10 coloured groups of flowers.   10s 6d

59   —THE GREENHOUSE.   *Post 8vo, original cloth.*   1838.   With coloured title page and 17 coloured plates.   15s

60   LITHOGRAPHIC COLOURED FLOWERS with Botanical Descriptions drawn and coloured by a lady.   *Folio, half calf.*   1826.   With 40 very attractive coloured plates of flowers, in brilliant state.   £7 10s

61   PAUL WILLIAM. § THE ROSE GARDEN.   *4to, original cloth.*   1848.   With 15 fine coloured illustrations of roses.   £1 5s

62   THE FLOWERS OF SHAKESPEARE.   *4to, morocco, gilt, gilt edges.*   N.D. (1840).   With 30 coloured groups of flowers to illustrate Shakespearean quotations.   £1 10s

63   MORRIS, R. § FLORA CONSPICUA.   A selection of the most ornamental plants for embellishing flower gardens and pleasure grounds.   *8vo, original boards.*   1830.   With 60 very finely drawn and coloured plates.   £3 3s

64   MARTYN, J., F.R.S. § THE ECLOGUES OF VIRGIL an English translation and notes.   With an appendix of plants mentioned in the Eclogues with 37 coloured plates.   *Royal 8vo, half calf, gilt.*   1813.   £3

65   WATSON, P. W. § DENDROLOGIA BRITANNICA or Trees and Shrubs that will live in the open air of Britain throughout the year.   2 volumes.   *8vo, half calf.*   1825.   With 180 coloured plates.   £3 10s

66   KNOWLES, G. B. & WESTCOTT, F. § THE FLORAL CABINET and magazine of Exotic Botany.   3 volumes.   *4to, half morocco.*   With 134 coloured plates.   1837–40.   £5 5s

67   MAUND, B. & HENSLOW, J. S. § THE BOTANIST.   5 volumes.   *Small 4to, half calf, gilt, marbled sides and edges.*   N.D. (1840).   With 240 coloured plates.   £5 17s 6d

68   THE BRITISH FLORIST.   6 volumes.   *Post 8vo, original cloth.*   Somewhat worn.   1846.   With 81 coloured plates.   Title pages slightly foxed but otherwise in fine condition.   £3 15s

69   MRS. LOUDON. § LADIES' MAGAZINE OF GARDENING.   *8vo morocco, gilt, gilt edges.*   1842.   With 12 coloured plates and many woodcuts.   12s 6d

70   TWINING, ELIZABETH. § ILLUSTRATIONS OF THE NATURAL ORDERS OF PLANTS with groups and description reduced from the original folio edition.   2 volumes.   *Royal 8vo, original cloth, gilt, gilt edges.*   1868.   With 160 coloured lithographs of flower groups.   A fine copy.   £2

71   BATEMAN, J. § A MONOGRAPH OF ODONTOGLOSSUM.   *Atlas folio, buckram, gilt edges.*   1874.   With 30 coloured plates of orchids.   £8 10s

72   —A SECOND CENTURY OF ORCHIDACEOUS PLANTS.   *4to, half calf.*   Worn.   1867.   With 100 coloured plates of orchids.   £5

73   BAXTER, W. § BRITISH PHÆNOGAMOUS BOTANY or figures and description of the genera of British Flowering Plants.   2 volumes.   *8vo, cloth.*   With 160 coloured plates of flowers.   1834–5.   £1

74   WATSON, W. & BEAN, W. § ORCHIDS.   Their culture and management with descriptions of all the kinds in general cultivation.   *8vo, cloth, top edge gilt.*   With 12 coloured plates and many other illustrations.   N.D. (1890).   8s 6d

75   MINER, H. S. § ORCHIDS: THE ROYAL FAMILY OF PLANTS.   With illustrations from Nature.   *Folio, original cloth, gilt edges.*   With 24 coloured plates.   A fine copy.   1885.   £1 5s

76   DE PUYOT, E. § LES ORCHIDÉES.   Histoire Iconographique.   Ouvrage ornée de 244 vignettes et de 50 chromolithographies (coloured).   *Royal 8vo, roan, gilt edges.*   A fine copy.   1880.   £1 10s

77   WEBER, J. C. § DIE ALPEN-PFLANZEN Deutchlands und der Schweiz.   4 volumes.   *12mo, original cloth, gilt.*   Munich 1872.   With 400 coloured plates of Alpine flowers.   £1 10s

78 WOOSTER, D. § ALPINE PLANTS. 2 volumes. *Royal 8vo, original cloth.* 1874. (Volume 1, 2nd edition). Spotless copies: with 108 coloured illustrations. £1 17s 6d

79 TWAMLEY, L. A. § THE ROMANCE OF NATURE. *8vo, pictorial morocco, gilt, gilt edges.* 1836. With coloured title page depicting a vase of flowers and 26 coloured plates. £1 10s

80 HEY, MRS. § THE MORAL OF FLOWERS. *8vo, half morocco, top edge gilt.* 1833. With 24 fine coloured plates. £1 10s

81 THE SPIRIT OF THE WOODS. *8vo, half morocco, top edge gilt.* 1837. With 26 coloured plates. £1 5s

82 HOSTEIN H. § FLORE DES DAMES OU NOUVEAU LANGAGE DES FLEURS. *12mo, morocco, gilt, gilt edges.* Paris, N.D. (1835). With 12 coloured groups of flowers. 10s 6d

83 BROOK'S CULPEPPER'S HERBAL IMPROVED. *Post 8vo, original cloth gilt.* N.D. (1840). With 29 coloured plates. 12s 6d

84 TYAS, R. § THE SENTIMENT OF FLOWERS or Language of Flora. 9th (large paper) edition. *8vo, morocco, gilt extra.* Floral designs in gilt on sides. 1842. With 29 plates containing 170 figures of plants carefully drawn and beautifully coloured. £1 10s

85 TWAMLEY, L. A. § OUR WILD FLOWERS. *8vo, morocco, gilt extra.* 1839. With 12 coloured groups of flowers. 10s 6d

86 TYAS, R. § THE SENTIMENT OF FLOWERS. *12mo, morocco, gilt, gilt edges.* A charming copy. 1839. With 12 coloured groups of flowers. 10s 6d

87 FLORA & THALIA or Gems of Flowers and Poetry, by a Lady. *12mo, vellum, gilt edges.* A mint copy. 1835. With 26 coloured plates. 12s 6d

88 DENNE-BARON, P. § FLEURS POETIQUES. *12mo, half morocco.* 1825. With 16 coloured plates. 8s 6d

89 ZACCONE, P. § NOUVEAU LANGAGE DES FLEURS. *Post 8vo, original boards,* 1855. With 18 coloured plates. 8s 6d

90 MILLER, T. § THE POETICAL LANGUAGE OF FLOWERS. *Post 8vo, original cloth, gilt.* 1861. With 8 coloured groups. 7s 6d

91 THE BOTANICAL KEEPSAKE. *Post 8vo, watered silk, gilt edges.* 1846. With 28 coloured plates. 10s 6d

92 CONVERSATIONS ON BOTANY. *Post 8vo, half morocco.* 1817. With 20 coloured plates. 12s 6d

93 THE CHRISTIAN GARLAND. *Post 8vo, cloth, gilt edges.* With 8 groups of flowers &c., printed in colours by Kronheim. Very charming. N.D. (1858). 8s 6d

94 THE CORONAL. *Post 8vo, cloth, gilt edges.* With 8 groups of flowers, birds &c., printed in colours by Kronheim, including a plate of Niagara Falls. 1858. 8s 6d

95 FLOWERS FROM MANY LANDS. A Christian companion for hours of recreation. *Post 8vo, cloth, gilt edges.* With 8 fine Kronheim plates of flowers (2 of American flowers). N.D. 1850. 8s 6d

96 FLOWERS FROM THE HOLY LAND by ROBERT TYAS. *Post 8vo, original cloth, gilt.* 1851. With 12 coloured groups. 8s 6d

97 FLOWERS AND HERALDRY, by ROBERT TYAS. *Post 8vo, original cloth, gilt,* 1851. With 24 emblazoned plates drawn and coloured by James Andrews. 12s 6d

98 THE YOUNG BOTANISTS in 13 dialogues. *12mo, boards, calf back.* 1810. With 12 coloured plates, some slightly foxed. 7s 6d

Books on American Birds, &c.

99 AUDUBON, J. J. § THE BIRDS OF AMERICA from drawings made in the United States and their territories. 8 volumes. *Royal 8vo, half roan, marbled sides and edges.* A fine set. New York N.D. The first octavo edition of this famous book. £42 10s

100 LEVAILLANT, F. § HISTOIRE NATURELLE d'une partie d' Oiseaux Nouveaux et rares de L'AMERIQUE ET DES INDES. Volume I (all issued). *4to, half calf, a little rubbed.* 1801. With 49 coloured plates. A few pages slightly affected by offset from the plates and one or two leaves repaired, but on the whole a good copy of this rare book. £25

101 WILSON, ALEXANDER. § AMERICAN ORNITHOLOGY OR THE NATURAL HISTORY OF THE BIRDS OF THE UNITED STATES. Illustrated with plates engraved and coloured from original drawings taken from nature. 9 volumes; and BONAPARTE, CHARLES LUCIAN. § THE NATURAL HISTORY OF BIRDS INHABITING THE UNITED STATES NOT GIVEN BY WILSON. 3 volumes. In all 12 volumes in 4. *Folio, 14½ by 11 ins, beautifully bound in dark green velvet.* Brass corners, worked in a design, and on front and back of each volume a coat of arms: the Royal Arms of Great Britain, quartered with the arms of Saxe-Meiningen, most delicately worked; the whole surrounded by a design and surmounted by a crown. The edges of the volumes superbly gilded in an intricate pattern. Each volume is contained in a dark green morocco folding case, lettered on back. Illustrated with 97 magnificently coloured plates, showing 350 species of birds. 1808–25.   £65

102 WILSON, A. & BONAPARTE, PRINCE CHARLES. § AMERICAN ORNITHOLOGY. 3 volumes. *Royal 8vo, half morocco, gilt, gilt tops.* A fine set. N.D. (1875). With portrait and 97 coloured plates of birds.   £4 10s

103 BAIRD, S. C. § THE BIRDS OF NORTH AMERICA, the descriptions of species based chiefly on the collections in the Museum of the Smithsonian Institute. 2 volumes. *4to, original cloth.* Philadelphia 1860. With 100 coloured plates of birds not given in Audubon, thus forming a valuable appendix to that work.   £16 16s

104 DE KAY, J. § NATURAL HISTORY OF NEW YORK. Part II: Birds (complete in itself). *4to original cloth.* Albany, 1844. With 120 coloured plates of birds.   £15

105 CATESBY, M. § PISCIUM, SERPENTUM INSECTORUM IMAGINES. The German edition of volume 2 of the Natural History of Carolina, Baltimore and the Bahamas, perhaps the most famous book on American Natural History. *Large folio, half calf.* Nuremberg 1777. With 109 coloured plates including an appendix of 9 plates only found in this edition: fishes, snakes, insects and other animals are given together with many of the plants of the country. The book, which is a rare one, is in very fine state.   £17 10s

105A HAHN, C. W. § VOEGEL AUS ASIEN, AFRICA, AMERICA UND NEU HOLLAND. *4to, original 5 parts.* Nuremberg, 1818–19. Complete with text and 30 coloured plates.   £3 15s

Some interesting French and German Bird Books

106 TEMMINCK, C. J. § LES PIGEONS par MADAME KNIP née Pauline de Courcelles, premier peintre d'histoire naturelle de S. M. l'Impératrice Reine Marie-Louise. Le texte par C. J. Temminck. *Large folio, full levant morocco, gilt, gilt edges.* A superb copy. With 87 magnificent coloured plates of pigeons. A few leaves and one or two plates are slightly foxed but otherwise in fine state throughout. Paris 1811. The texture of the plates is superior even to those of Levaillant.   £55

107 MEYER, J. D. § VORSTELLUNGEN ALLERHAND THIERE. 3 volumes in 2. *Folio, vellum.* A handsome copy. With beautiful illuminated title pages, and 240 charming and interesting coloured plates of birds, animals and fishes, showing their anatomy. Nuremberg, 1748–52. A very rare book in mint state.   £60

108 LESSON, R. P. § HISTOIRE NATURELLE DES OISEAUX DE PARADIS ET DES EPIMAQUES. *Small folio, half calf.* Paris N.D. (1830) with 43 magnificent coloured plates of birds of paradise.   £12 12s

109 LESSON, R. P. § HISTOIRE NATURELLE DES OISEAUX MOUCHES ET DES COLIBRIS. 3 volumes. *Half morocco, gilt, gilt edges.* A handsome set. 1830–2. With 218 coloured plates of humming birds.   £9 9s

110 LESSON, R. P. § HISTOIRE NATURELLE DES OISEAUX-MOUCHES. *8vo, half morocco, gilt, gilt top.* Paris N.D. (1830). With 85 brilliant plates of humming birds.   £3 15s

111 SCHAEFFER, J. C. § ELEMENTA ORNITHOLOGICA ICONIBUS, vivis coloribus expressis illustrata. *4to, half green morocco, marbled boards, uncut.* Ratisbon (Regensburg) 1779. With 70 coloured plates of birds.   £4 10s

112 SALERNE, M. § HISTOIRE NATURELLE DES OISEAUX. *4to contemporary morocco, gilt.* A finely tooled binding though back faded. *Gilt edges.* Paris 1767. With beautiful coloured frontispiece depicting falconry and 31 fine coloured plates of birds. A very handsome book.   £12 10s

113 BUFFON, G. LE CLERC. § OEUVRES COMPLETES.   Edited by LACEPEDE.   12 volumes with supplement 5 volumes.   In all 17 volumes.   *8vo, diced calf.*   A fine set with over 320 coloured plates.   Paris 1817–19.   £7 10s

114 —HISTOIRE NATURELLE.   54 volumes.   *Post 8vo, contemporary tree calf.*   A fine set.   1785 &c.   With over 200 coloured plates of birds and animals.   £4 4s

115 VON JACQUIN J. F. E. § GESCHICHTE DER VÖGEL.   *4to boards.*   Vienna 1784.   With 19 charming coloured plates of birds.   Scarce.   £2

116 SCHINTZ. § NATURGESCHICHTE DER VÖGEL.   *Small folio, roan.*   Zurich, 1853.   Very attractively illustrated with 124 coloured lithographs of birds, brilliantly performed.   £10

117 SUNDEVALL, G. J. § SVENSKA FOGLARNA.   2 volumes.   *Oblong folio, half morocco, gilt edges.*   Volume 1 text, Volume 2 contains 84 fine coloured plates of the birds of Sweden, several birds to a plate.   1856.   £3

118 DE CHERVILLE, G. § LES OISEAUX DE CHASSE.   *Small 4to, half red calf.*   34 coloured lithographs of game-birds.   Fine copy.   N.D. (1860).   15s

British Bird Books

119 ALBIN, ELEAZAR. § A NATURAL HISTORY OF BIRDS.   2 volumes.   *4to contemporary calf, rebacked.*   1738.   With 205 copper plates 'curiously engraved from the life and excellently coloured by the author'.   £10 10s

120 EDWARDS, G. § A NATURAL HISTORY OF UNCOMMON BIRDS.   4 volumes and GLEANINGS OF NATURAL HISTORY, 3 volumes, 7 volumes in 4.   *4to tree calf, rebacked.*   1743–5.   With coloured frontispiece and 361 coloured plates.   A fine set.   £25

121 HAYES, W. § A NATURAL HISTORY OF BRITISH BIRDS with their portraits accurately drawn and beautifully coloured from nature.   *Large folio, boards.*   1775.   With 40 fine coloured engravings.   £15

122 —PORTRAITS OF RARE AND CURIOUS BIRDS WITH THEIR DESCRIPTIONS from the menagery of Osterley Park in the County of Middlesex.   *4to, contemporary scarlet morocco, gilt, gilt edges.*   A fine copy.   1794.   With 100 brilliantly coloured plates.   £10 10s

123 LEWIN, W. § BIRDS OF GREAT BRITAIN, systematically arranged, accurately engraved and painted from nature.   8 volumes in 4.   *4to, half morocco, gilt tops.*   1796–1800.   With 267 coloured plates of birds and 59 of their eggs.   A handsome and comprehensive work.   £12 10s

124 SHAW, G. & NODDER, F. P. § THE NATURALISTS' MISCELLANY or coloured figures of natural objects drawn and described immediately from nature.   24 volumes in 12.   *8vo, contemporary half straight-grained morocco, gilt.*   A very fine set.   With 1,064 coloured plates of birds, fishes, butterflies and shells &c., 1790.   A perfect copy of this book is quite unusual.   £20

125 MARTYN, W. F. § A NEW DICTIONARY OF NATURAL HISTORY and complete universal display of animated nature.   2 volumes.   *Folio, half calf, gilt.*   1785.   With 100 unusual plates of birds, fish &c., several varieties on each plate.   £5 5s

126 MILLER, J. F. § CIMELIA PHYSICA, Figures of Rare and Curious Quadrupeds, Birds, &c., together with several of the most elegant Plants.   Engraved and coloured from the subjects themselves.   With descriptions by George Shaw.   *Folio, 21 by 14 ins, half crimson morocco, gilt edges.*   With 60 beautifully coloured plates, mainly of birds.   1796.   £11 11s

127 THE BRITISH ZOOLOGY.   Published under the inspection of the Cymmrodorion Society, instituted for the promoting of useful charities and the knowledge of Nature among the Descendants of the Ancient Britons.   Illustrated with 107 copper plates, beautifully coloured: 9 of animals and the remainder of birds.   *Folio, 21 by 14 ins, half calf.*   Rather worn, but all the text and plates in fine condition.   1766.   £18 18s

128 BROWN, PETER. § NEW ILLUSTRATIONS OF ZOOLOGY.   Containing 50 coloured plates of new, curious and nondescript birds with a few quadrupeds, reptiles and insects, together with a short and scientific description of the same.   *Quarto, calf.*   A fine copy.   1776.   £7 10s

129 SWAINSON, W. § ZOOLOGICAL ILLUSTRATIONS or original figures of new, rare and interesting animals, selected chiefly from the classes of Ornithology, Entomology and Conchology.   2 volumes.   *8vo. Contemporary straight-grained crimson morocco, gilt, gilt edges.*   A very fine copy.   With 183 coloured plates of birds, butterflies and shells, brilliantly executed and in spotless condition.   1820–2.   £8 8s

130 DONOVAN, E. § THE NATURAL HISTORY OF BRITISH BIRDS. 10 volumes in 5. *8vo, contemporary calf.* New joints. 1799–1819 with 244 coloured plates.   £10 10s

131 HILL, JOHN. § AN HISTORY OF ANIMALS, containing descriptions of the birds, beasts, fishes and insects of the several parts of the world. *Folio, contemporary calf, gilt.* 1752. With 28 coloured copper plates.
£4

132 PENNANT, T. § INDIAN ZOOLOGY. *4to, rebound half calf, uncut.* 2nd edition, 1790. With coloured title page and 16 coloured plates.   £3 10s

133 CUVIER, BARON. § THE ANIMAL KINGDOM. 8 volumes *8vo, diced calf.* A fine set. 1834. With over 600 coloured plates of birds, fish, animals &c.   £3 10s

134 THE ANIMAL KINGDOM. 16 volumes. *Royal 8vo, half morocco, calf sides, gilt edges.* A beautiful copy. 1827–34. With hundreds of very fine coloured plates (150 of birds and 60 of fish).   £7 10s

135 LEAR, E. § ILLUSTRATIONS OF THE FAMILY OF PSITTACIDÆ OR PARROTS. The greater part of them species hitherto unfigured. Containing 42 lithographic plates (finely coloured), drawn from life and on stone. *Folio 21 by 14 ins, full crimson morocco gilt, gilt edges.* A spotless copy. 1832 £18 18s

136 BOLTON, JAMES. § HARMONIA RURALIS, or an Essay towards a natural history of BRITISH SONG BIRDS. 2 volumes in 1. *Small folio, 13 by 9 ins. Magnificently bound in full crimson straight-grained morocco, gilt, gilt edges.* A superb copy, with 90 coloured plates of birds and their nests and eggs, most delicately drawn and coloured. 1794.
£7 7s

137 —Another edition. 2 volumes in 1. *12 by 9½ ins, half roan, marbled sides, top edge gilt, other edges uncut.* A later edition published in 1830, but with the same 80 plates finely coloured.   £5 5s

138 GREENE, W. T. § PARROTS IN CAPTIVITY. 3 volumes. *Royal 8vo, original cloth, gilt tops.* 1884–7. With 81 coloured plates. One or two slightly spotted, but in the main in fine state.   £4

139 MUDIE, R. § THE FEATHERED TRIBES OF THE BRITISH ISLES. 2 volumes. *Half calf.* 1834. With Baxter frontispieces (rather foxed) and 18 coloured plates.   £1

140 —Another edition. 1841. *Cloth, gilt.* With frontispieces and 18 coloured plates.   15s

141 NATURAL HISTORY OF BIRDS. *12mo, morocco, gilt, gilt edges.* Very fine copy. With Baxter plate in colours and many woodcuts. 1834.   6s

142 MORRIS, B. R. § BRITISH GAME BIRDS AND WILDFOWL. *4to, half morocco, gilt, gilt top.* 1864. With 69 coloured plates.   £2

143 A TREATISE ON BRITISH SONG BIRDS. *8vo, half calf.* 1823. With 15 coloured engravings. Very charming.   £1 5s

144 GOSSE, P. H. § POPULAR BRITISH ORNITHOLOGY. *Pocket 4to, cloth.* 1849. With 20 coloured plates.   15s

145 JARDINE, SIR W. § THE NATURAL HISTORY OF HUMMING BIRDS. 2 volumes in 1. *Post 8vo, morocco gilt (worn), gilt edges.* With 64 coloured plates. N.D. (1840).   15s

146 MORRIS, REV. F. O. § A HISTORY OF BRITISH BIRDS. 6 volumes. *Royal 8vo, original cloth.* Over 350 coloured plates. 1851–7.   £3 10s

147 SWAYSLAND, W. § FAMILIAR WILD BIRDS. 4 volumes. *Post 8vo, original pictorial cloth, gilt, gilt edges,* 1883. With 200 coloured plates of birds. A useful and attractive book.   £1 10s

148 MEYER, H. L. § COLOURED ILLUSTRATIONS OF BRITISH BIRDS AND THEIR EGGS. 7 volumes. *8vo, half morocco, gilt.* Fine set. 1842–50. With 432 coloured plates.   £6 10s

Select Bibliography

A BIBLIOGRAPHY CAN BE a fairly serious and academic affair, or at the other extreme it can be what amounts to a list for further reading. Since the readers of this book may well vary from those with an interest in the subject, but little real knowledge, to those who have spent a lifetime in contact with rare books, I will endeavour to please both parties by saying something, first, in the form of a bibliographical note from a professional viewpoint, followed by a list of books to give pleasure to the more general reader while adding to his knowledge.

THERE HAS ALWAYS BEEN a notable lack of reference works to help the collector of old natural history books. When I started to sell them in 1930 I had no assistance except for Pretzel, an unreadable and unhelpful German book, so I had to go it alone and keep all my old catalogues. In 1938 Gordon Dunthorne published in Washington, USA, *Flower and Fruit Prints of the Eighteenth and Early Nineteenth Centuries*. I was then quite a young man and it seemed to me, in my arrogance, rather poor; but I was wrong and often consult it now. It was, however, fairly limited in its scope.

In the 1950s many more books were produced to aid the bibliophile, and I must give first place to Nissen's *Die Botanische Buchillustration*. The first edition of this essential work came out just before the Second World War, and was therefore almost unknown outside Germany. The second edition (2 vols, Stuttgart, 1951–2) was and still is the best bibliography of flower books. Nissen's work on bird books (*Die Illustrierten Vogelbücher*, 1953) was, I think, not as good as some of the books produced in England, but the third part of his massive undertaking, *Die Zoologische Buchillustration* (second and better edition, 1969), is required reading for all who have a serious interest in books on animals, fish, shells and insects.

In the 1950s some very good and useful books came out in England, in all of which I had some part. For the existence of these works we must thank George Rainbird, who commissioned and produced them, and the late Sir William Collins, a wonderful man and a lifelong friend, who published them.

Thornton's Temple of Flora came out in 1951. The literary introduction was written by Geoffrey Grigson and I compiled the bibliography, while William Stearn wrote a page of botanical notes. It is obviously much easier to write a full account of one book than of many, and while *The Temple of Flora* is perhaps the most complicated of all natural history books, this point must be stressed. It is now out of print, but all Thornton-lovers should try at least to see a copy.

Fine Bird Books was published in 1953. The literary part was written by Sacheverell Sitwell, and the bibliography was the work of James Fisher and me. At the time I thought I had produced a good bibliography, but James Fisher discovered a number of books that I had omitted. Our joint achievement is still unequalled.

The *Album de Redouté* by Roger Madol, Sacheverell Sitwell and William Stearn came out a year later, in 1954. Monsieur Madol, having appeared before a selection committee of George Rainbird, Billy Collins and me, was commissioned to prepare the bibliography. Like all of us, he left some gaps, and I attempted to fill in these *lacunae*. I had only just, as I thought, finished this task when, both fortunately (for the book) and unfortunately (for me), we discovered that William Stearn had been working on this very project for a large part of his life. The result of our combined efforts was splendid.

In *Great Flower Books*, published in 1956, the literary part was once again the work of Sachie Sitwell and Wilfrid Blunt, and the bibliography was edited by Patrick Synge. I had been asked to prepare the bibliography, but I felt that I had learnt my lesson on the *Album de Redouté* and *Fine Bird Books*. William Stearn and Sabine Wilson did all the real catalogue work, but I was asked to go over it and see what I could add. As always, a number of minds seemed to produce a better result, and the book is a very good one, although from a purely workaday viewpoint Nissen's *Die Botanische Buchillustration* contains more actual material.

I was very proud to be the only person to be associated with all four of these books, which are essential for the collector but which are, sadly, now out of print and worth many times their original published price.

As a final point, before going on to the list of more general books, some of which are very good, it is worth noting that the catalogues (together with the price lists) of book auctioneers, of whom the most notable are Sotheby's and Christie's, have always been of immense bibliographical assistance. In a humbler but still important way, so have booksellers' catalogues.

THE FOLLOWING IS A SELECTION of biographies and other books on natural history illustration which have appeared in recent years.

Blunt, Wilfrid and William T. Stearn, *The Art of Botanical Illustration*, 1950

Blunt, Wilfrid and William T. Stearn, *The Compleat Naturalist: A Life of Linnaeus*, 1977

Calmann, Gerta, *Ehret: Flower Painter Extraordinary*, 1977

Chancellor, John, *Audubon*, 1978

Coats, Alice M., *The Book of Flowers: Four Centuries of Flower Illustration*, 1973

Coats, Alice M., *The Treasury of Flowers*, 1975

Dance, Peter, *The Art of Natural History: Animal Illustrators and Their Work*, 1978

Dixon, Joan M. (commentary by), *Gould's Mammals*, 1977

Jenkins, Alan, *The Naturalists*, 1978

Lysaght, A.M., *The Book of Birds: Five Centuries of Bird Illustration*, 1975

Sepp, Jan Christiaan, *Butterflies and Moths* (engravings by Christiaan Sepp and his son Jan Christiaan, with a text by Stuart McNeill), 1978

Illustrations

Place of publication is London unless stated otherwise.

Cereus. British Museum (Natural History).

44 Jean Louis Prévost: *Collection des Fleurs et des Fruits Peints d'après Nature . . . avec une Explication des Planches par Ant. Nic Duchesne*, large folio, Paris, 1805. Plate 9. Royal Horticultural Society, Lindley Library, photo Angelo Hornak.

45 Jean Louis Prévost: *Collection des Fleurs et des Fruits . . . .* Plate 42. Royal Horticultural Society, Lindley Library, photo Angelo Hornak.

46 George Brookshaw: *Pomona Britannica, or, A Collection of the Most Esteemed Fruits at Present Cultivated in this Country . . . Selected Principally from the Royal Gardens at Hampton Court . . . Accurately Drawn and Coloured from Nature, with Full Descriptions . . . ,* 1804–12. Melon. Weidenfeld and Nicolson Archives, photographed at Bernard Quaritch Ltd.

47 Pierre-Joseph Redouté: *Choix des Plus Belles Fleurs Prises dans Différentes Familles du Règne Végétal et de Quelques Branches des Plus Beaux Fruits, Groupées Quelquefois, et Souvent Animées par des Insectes et des Papillons*, folio, Paris, 1827–33. *Tulipe de Gesner.* British Museum (Natural History).

48 Pierre-Joseph Redouté: *Les Liliacées*, 8 vols, folio, Paris, 1802–16. Vol. IV, *Iris Monnieri.* Weidenfeld and Nicolson Archives, photographed by Angelo Hornak at Bernard Quaritch Ltd.

50 Augustin Pyramus de Candolle: *Plantarum Succulentarum Historia ou Histoire Naturelle des Plantes Grasses*, 2 vols, folio, Paris, 1798–1829. Plate 14, *Aloë rhodacantha.* British Museum (Natural History).

51 Etienne Pierre Ventenat: *Jardin de la Malmaison*, 2 vols, folio, Paris, 1803–5. *Hibiscus heterophyllus.* British Museum (Natural History).

52 Gerrit van Spaëndonck: *Fleurs Dessinées d'après Nature*, folio, Paris, 1801. Lavatera. British Museum (Natural History).

53 Pierre-Joseph Redouté: *Les Roses*, 3 vols, folio, Paris, 1817–24. *Rosa turbinata.* British Museum (Natural History).

54 Aimé Jacques Alexandre Bonpland: *Descriptions des Plantes Rares Cultivées à Malmaison et à Navarre*, folio, Paris, 1813–17. Plate 36, *Cactus ambiguus.* British Museum (Natural History).

55 Ambroise Marie François Joseph Palisot de Beauvois: *Plantes d'Oware et de Bénin, en Afrique*, 2 vols, folio, Paris, 1804. *Ventenatia glauca.* British Museum (Natural History).

56 Giorgio Gallesio: *Pomona Italiana, ossia Trattato degli Alberi Fruttiferi*, 2 vols, folio, Pisa, 1817–39. *Pesca Carota.* British Museum (Natural History).

57 J. Antoine Risso and Pierre Antoine Poiteau: *Histoire Naturelle des Orangers*, folio, Paris, 1818–20. Plate 56, Bergamotte. British Museum (Natural History).

58 Samuel Curtis: *A Monograph of the Genus Camellia*, folio, 1819. Single White and Single Red Camellias. Library of the Royal Botanic Gardens, Kew, photo Angelo Hornak.

60 William Paul Crillon Barton: *A Flora of North America, Illustrated by Coloured Figures Drawn from Nature*, 3 vols, 4to, Philadelphia, 1821–3. Plate 41, *Tradescantia Virginica.* Weidenfeld and Nicolson Archives, photographed by Angelo Hornak at Bernard Quaritch Ltd.

61 Michel Etienne Descourtilz: *Flore Pittoresque et Médicale des Antilles, ou Histoire Naturelle des Plantes Usuelles des Colonies Françaises, Anglaises, Espagnoles et Portugaises, Peinte d'après les Dessins Faits sur les Lieux*, 8 vols, 8vo, Paris, 1821–9. Plate 62, *Grenadille sans Franges.* British Museum (Natural History).

62 Arsenne Thiébaut de Bernaud: *Traités Elémentaire de Botanique*, 4to, Paris, 1837. Plate 24, *Fougères.* Weidenfeld and Nicolson Archives, photographed by Angelo Hornak at Bernard Quaritch Ltd.

63 Joseph Dalton Hooker: *The Rhododendrons of Sikkim-Himalaya . . . from Drawings and Descriptions Made on the Spot . . . ,* 3 parts, folio, 1849–51. Plate 3, *Rhododendron barbatum.* British Museum (Natural History).

65 Samuel Curtis: *The Beauties of Flora, Being a Selection of Flowers Painted from Nature . . . ,* folio, Gamston, Notts, 1806–20. Plate 10, Dahlias. Royal Horticultural Society, Lindley Library, photo Angelo Hornak.

66 John Sibthorp and James Edward Smith: *Flora Graeca; sive Plantarum Rariorum Historia, quas in Provinciis aut Insuliis Graeciae Legit, Investigavit et Depingi Curavit*, 10 vols, folio, 1806–40. Title page to Vol. IX. British Museum (Natural History).

67 John Buonarotti Papworth: *Ornamental Gardening*, 4to, 1823. Plate 14, A Woodland Seat. Weidenfeld and Nicolson Archives, photographed by Angelo Hornak at Bernard Quaritch Ltd.

68 Thomas Andrew Knight: *Pomona Herefordiensis; Containing Coloured Engravings of the Old Cider and Perry Fruits of Herefordshire . . . Accompanied with a Descriptive Account of Each Variety*, 4to, 1811. Plate 8, The Orange Pippin. Weidenfeld and Nicolson Archives, photographed by Angelo Hornak at Bernard Quaritch Ltd.

69 Mrs Edward Bury: *A Selection of Hexandrian Plants Belonging to the Natural Orders Amaryllidae and Liliaceae . . . ,* large folio, 1831–4. Plate 11, *Crinum pedunculatum.* Weidenfeld and Nicolson Archives, photographed by Angelo Hornak at Bernard Quaritch Ltd.

70 James Bateman: *The Orchidaceae of Mexico and Guatemala*, large folio, 1837–43. Plate 17, *Epidendrum*

Macrochilum var. Roseum. British Museum (Natural History).

71 William Roscoe: *Monandrian Plants of the Order Scitaminee, Chiefly Drawn from Living Specimens . . .*, 2 vols, folio, Liverpool, 1824–9. Weidenfeld and Nicolson Archives, photographed by Angelo Hornak at Bernard Quaritch Ltd.

72 Lorenzo Berlèse: *Iconographie du Genre Caméllia ou Description et Figures des Caméllia les Plus Beaux et les Plus Rares Peints d'après Nature*, 3 vols, folio, Paris, 1839–43. *Camellia Ventustissima*. British Museum (Natural History).

74 Mrs Jane Loudon: *The Ladies' Flower Garden of Ornamental Bulbous Plants*, 4to, 1841. Plate 12, Gladioli. British Museum (Natural History).

75 Elizabeth Twining: *Illustrations of the Natural Orders of Plants. Arranged in Groups; with Descriptions*, 2 vols, folio, 1849–55. The Mallow Tribe. Weidenfeld and Nicolson Archives, photographed at Bernard Quaritch Ltd.

76 Mary Elizabeth Rosenberg: *The Museum of Flowers*, royal 8vo, 1845. Plate 1, Anemones. Weidenfeld and Nicolson Archives, photographed by Angelo Hornak at Bernard Quaritch Ltd.

78 Eleazar Albin: *A Natural History of Birds with 306 Copper Plates, Curiously Engraven from the Life, and Exactly Coloured by the Author, Eleazar Albin. To Which Are Added, Notes and Observations by W. Derham*, 3 vols, 4to, 1731–8. Plate 56, Grosbeak. British Museum (Natural History).

79 Mark Catesby: *The Natural History of Carolina, Florida and the Bahama Islands: Containing the Figures of Birds, Beasts, Fishes, Serpents, Insects, and Plants: Particularly, the Forest-Trees, Shrubs, and Other Plants, not Hitherto Described, or Very Incorrectly Figured by Authors. Together with Their Descriptions in English and French. To Which Are Added Observations on the Air, Soil and Waters; with Remarks upon Agriculture, Grain, Pulse, Roots etc . . .*, 2 vols, large folio, 1731–43. Plate 100, White-Faced Teal. British Museum (Natural History).

80 Albertus Seba: *Locupletissimi Rerum Naturalium Thesauri Accurata Descriptio, et Iconibus Artificiosissimis Expressio, per Universam Physices Historiam*, 4 vols, large folio, Amsterdam, 1734–65. Plate 67. British Museum (Natural History).

81 Cornelis Nozeman and others: *Nederlandsche Vogelen; Volgens Hunne Huishoding, Aert en Eigenschaften*, 5 vols, large folio, Amsterdam, 1770–1829. Cuckoo. British Museum (Natural History).

83 George Edwards: *A Natural History (A Natural History of Uncommon Birds, and of Some Other Rare and Undescribed Animals, Quadrupedes, Reptiles, Fishes,*

Insects, etc., Exhibited in Two Hundred and Ten Copper-Plates, from Designs Copied Immediately from Nature, and Curiously Coloured After Life. . . . and *Gleanings of Natural History . . .* large folio, 1802–5 (1st edition 7 vols, 4to, 1743–64). Plate 87, Purple Water Hen. Weidenfeld and Nicolson Archives, photographed by Angelo Hornak at Bernard Quaritch Ltd.

84 Thomas Pennant: *The British Zoology. Class 1: Quadrupeds. Class 11: Birds. Published under the Inspection of the Cymmrodorion Society, Instituted for the Promoting of Useful Charities, and the Knowledge of Nature, Among the Descendants of the Ancient Britons*, large folio, 1761–6. Group of Finches. Weidenfeld and Nicolson Archives, photographed by Angelo Hornak at Bernard Quaritch Ltd.

85 James Bolton: *Harmonia Ruralis; or, an Essay Towards a Natural History of British Song Birds: etc.*, 2 vols, 4to, Stannary (near Halifax, Yorkshire), 1794–6. Canary's Nest and Eggs. Weidenfeld and Nicolson Archives, photographed at Bernard Quaritch Ltd.

86 Edward Donovan: *The Natural History of British Birds; or a Selection of the Most Rare, Beautiful, and Interesting Birds Which Inhabit This Country: etc.*, 10 vols, 4to, 1794–1819. Plate 90, Little Owl. British Museum (Natural History).

87 William Hayes: *A Natural History of British Birds, etc., with Their Portraits, Accurately Drawn, and Beautifully Coloured from Nature*, large folio, 1771–5. Plate 11, Lapwing. British Museum (Natural History).

89 Captain Thomas Brown: *Illustrations of the American Ornithology of Alexander Wilson and Charles Lucian Bonaparte*, very large folio, Edinburgh, 1831–5. Honduras Turkey. Weidenfeld and Nicolson Archives, photographed by Angelo Hornak at Bernard Quaritch Ltd.

90 Xaviero Manetti and Giovanni Gerini: *Ornithologia Methodice Digesta atque Iconibus Aeneis ad Vivum Illuminatis Ornata (Storia Naturale degli Uccelli)*, 5 vols, large folio, Florence, 1767–76. Plate 7, Wood Duck. Weidenfeld and Nicolson Archives, photographed by Angelo Hornak at Bernard Quaritch Ltd from *Fine Bird Books*, George Rainbird/Collins, 1953, reproduced by permission of George Rainbird.

91 Johann Leonhard Frisch and others: *Vorstellung der Vögel in Teutschland und Beyläuffig auch Einiger Fremden, mit Ihren Eigenschaften Beschrieben . . . und nach Ihren Natürlichen Farben*, folio, Berlin, 1733–63. Cockerel. Weidenfeld and Nicolson Archives, photographed by Angelo Hornak at Bernard Quaritch Ltd from *Fine Bird Books*, George Rainbird/Collins, 1953, reproduced by permission of George Rainbird.

92 William Hayes: *Portraits of Rare and Curious Birds, with Their Descriptions, Accurately Drawn and Beautifully Coloured from Species in the Menagerie of Child, the Banker, at Osterley Park*, near London, 4to, 1794–9. Red Maccaw. Weidenfeld and Nicolson Archives, photographed by Angelo Hornak at Bernard Quaritch Ltd.

93 Edward Lear: *Illustrations of the Family of Psittacidae, or Parrots: The Greater Part of Them Species Hitherto Unfigured . . .* , large folio, 1830–2. Red-Capped Parrakeet. Weidenfeld and Nicolson Archives, photographed by Angelo Hornak at Bernard Quaritch Ltd.

94 John James Audubon: *The Birds of America from Original Drawings Made During a Residence of Twenty Five Years in the United States*, 4 vols, elephant folio, 1827–38. Plate 23, Blue Jays. Weidenfeld and Nicolson Archives, photographed by Angelo Hornak at Bernard Quaritch Ltd from *Fine Bird Books*, George Rainbird/Collins, 1953, reproduced by permission of George Rainbird.

95 Alexander Wilson: *American Ornithology; or, The Natural History of the Birds of the United States*, 9 vols, folio, Philadelphia, 1808–14. Plate 57, Woodpeckers. Weidenfeld and Nicolson Archives, photographed by Angelo Hornak at Bernard Quaritch Ltd from *Fine Bird Books*, George Rainbird/Collins, 1953, reproduced by permission of George Rainbird.

96 Jean Théodore Descourtilz: *Ornithologie Brésilienne ou Histoire des Oiseaux du Brésil, Remarquables par Leur Plumage, Leur Chant ou Leurs Habitudes*, large folio, Rio de Janeiro, 1854–6. Plate 27, *Tersina Coerulia*. British Museum (Natural History).

98 John Frederick Miller and George Shaw: *Cimelia Physica, Figures of Rare and Curious Quadrupeds, Birds &c. Together with Several of the Most Elegant Plants*, large folio, 1796. Plate 57, *Ramphastos Indicus*. British Museum (Natural History).

99 François Levaillant: *Histoire Naturelle d'une Partie d'Oiseaux Nouveaux et Rares de l'Amériques et des Indes*, Vol. 1 (all published), folio, Paris, 1801–2. Plate 25, *Le grand Cotinga*. British Museum (Natural History).

100 Jean-Baptiste Audebert and Louis Jean Pierre Viellot: *Oiseaux Dorés ou à Reflets Métalliques*, 2 vols, folio, Paris, 1802. Plate 55, *L'Oiseau Mouche à Ventre Gris*. British Museum (Natural History).

101 Louis Jean Pierre Viellot: *Histoire Naturelle des Plus Beaux Oiseaux Chanteurs de la Zone Torride*, large folio, Paris, 1805. Plate 70, *Paroare Huppé*. British Museum (Natural History).

102–3 Charles Lucien Bonaparte: *American Ornithology – Birds Not Given by Wilson*, 4 vols, folio, Philadelphia, 1825–33. Plate 26. British Museum (Natural History).

104 Johann Andreas Naumann: *Naturgeschichte der Vögel Deutschlands. Nach Eigenen Erfahrungen Entworfen . . .* , 13 vols, 8vo, Leipzig, 1822–60. *Naumanns Raubvögelfalle*. British Museum (Natural History).

105 John James Audubon: *The Birds of America from Original Drawings Made During a Residence of Twenty Five Years in the United States*, 4 vols, elephant folio, 1827–38. Plate 42, Orchard Oriole. British Museum (Natural History).

107 John James Audubon: *The Birds of America . . . .* Plate 181, Golden Eagle. British Museum (Natural History).

108–9 John James Audubon: *The Birds of America . . . .* Plate 281, Great White Heron. Christie, Manson and Wood.

110 John James Audubon: *The Birds of America . . . .* Plate 336, Yellow Crowned Heron. British Museum (Natural History).

113 René Primevère Lesson: *Histoire Naturelle des Oiseaux-Mouches, Ouvrage Orné de Planches Dessinées et Gravées par les Meilleurs Artistes, et Dédié à S.A.R. Mademoiselle*, 4to, Paris, 1828–30. Plate 27, *Oiseau-Mouche Sapho*. Weidenfeld and Nicolson Archives, photographed by Angelo Hornak at Bernard Quaritch Ltd.

114 John Gould: *The Birds of Australia*, 8 vols, large folio, 1840–69. Plate 13, *Roseate Cockatoo*. Weidenfeld and Nicolson Archives, photographed by Angelo Hornak at Bernard Quaritch Ltd from *Fine Bird Books*, George Rainbird/Collins, 1953, reproduced by permission of George Rainbird.

115 John Edward Gray: *Gleanings from the Menagerie and Aviary at Knowsley Hall*, large folio, Knowsley, 1846–50. Plate 14, Stanley Crane. Linnean Society Library, photo Angelo Hornak.

116 Comte Georges-Louis Leclerc de Buffon and others: *Histoire Naturelle des Oiseaux*, 10 vols, folio, Paris, 1770–86. Vol. II, Plate 121, Pheasant. British Museum (Natural History).

117 Philip Henry Gosse: *Illustrations of the Birds of Jamaica*, folio, 1849. *Tanagrella Rubicolla*. British Museum (Natural History).

118 Daniel Giraud Elliot: *A Monograph of the Paradiseidae or Birds of Paradise*, elephant folio, 1873. *Epimachus Ellioti*. Weidenfeld and Nicolson Archives, photographed by Angelo Hornak at Bernard Quaritch Ltd.

119 François Levaillant: *Histoire Naturelle des Perroquets*, 2 vols, large folio, Paris, 1801–5. Plate 127, *Première variété du grand Lori*. Weidenfeld and Nicolson Archives, photographed by Angelo Hornak at Bernard Quaritch Ltd.

120 Daniel Giraud Elliot: *A Monograph of the Phasianidae or Family of the Pheasants*, 2 vols, elephant

folio, New York, 1870–2. Black-Headed Tragopan.
Weidenfeld and Nicolson Archives, photographed by
Angelo Hornak at Bernard Quaritch Ltd from *Fine
Bird Books*, George Rainbird/Collins, 1953.

123 John James Audubon: *The Birds of America from
Original Drawings Made During a Residence of Twenty
Five Years in the United States*, 4 vols, elephant folio,
1827–38. Plate 311, American White Pelican.
Christie, Manson and Wood.

125 John Gould: *A Monograph of the Trochilidae, or
Family of Humming-Birds*, 6 vols, large folio, 1849–87.
Heliodoxa Jacula. Weidenfeld and Nicolson Archives,
photographed by Angelo Hornak at Bernard
Quaritch Ltd.

127 John Gould: *The Birds of Great Britain*, 5 vols,
large folio, 1862–73. Sparrow-Hawk. Weidenfeld
and Nicolson Archives, photographed by Angelo
Hornak at Bernard Quaritch Ltd.

128–9 Daniel Giraud Elliot: *A Monograph of the
Phasianidae or Family of the Pheasants*, 2 vols, elephant
folio, New York, 1870–2. *Argusianus Grayii*.
Weidenfeld and Nicolson Archives, photographed by
Angelo Hornak at Bernard Quaritch Ltd.

130 George Ernest Shelley: *A Monograph of the
Nectariniidae (Cinnyridae), or Family of Sun-Birds*, large
4to, 1876–80. *Cinnyris Mariquensis*. British Museum
(Natural History).

134–5 Marcus Elieser Bloch: *Ichtyologie ou Histoire
Naturelle, Générale et Particulière des Poissons*, 12 vols,
large folio, Berlin, 1785–97 (original German edition
1782–95). Plate 351, *Trigla Volitans*. Weidenfeld and
Nicolson Archives, photographed by Angelo Hornak
at Bernard Quaritch Ltd.

137 Christian Gottfried Ehrenberg: *Symbolae Physicae,
seu Icones et Descriptiones Corpurum Naturalium Novorum
aut Minus Cognitorum, quae ex Itinere per Libyam,
Aegyptum, Nubiam, Dongolam, Syriam, Arabiam et
Habessiniam P.C. Hemprich et C.G. Ehrenberg studio annis
1820–25 Redierunt*, 4 vols, folio, Berlin, 1828–45.
Plate 9, *Sciurus brachyotus*. Linnean Society Library,
photo Angelo Hornak.

138 above Marcus Elieser Bloch: *Ichtyologie ou
Histoire Naturelle, Générale et Particulière des Poissons*,
12 vols, large folio, Berlin, 1785–97. Plate 323, *Anthias
Formosus*. Weidenfeld and Nicolson Archives,
photographed by Angelo Hornak at Bernard
Quaritch Ltd.

138 below Mrs Sarah Bowdich: *The Freshwater Fishes
of Great Britain Drawn and Described*, 4to, 1828.
The Trout. Weidenfeld and Nicolson Archives,
photographed by Angelo Hornak at Bernard
Quaritch Ltd.

139 Louis Renard: *Poissons, Ecrévisses et Crabes de
Divers Couleurs, et Figures Extraordinaires que l'on Trouve

*Autour des Isles Moluques et sur les Côtes des Terres
Australes . . .* , folio, Amsterdam, 1754 (1st
edition 1718–19). Exotic fish. Weidenfeld and
Nicolson Archives, photographed at Bernard
Quaritch Ltd.

140–1 Charles Catton: *Animals Drawn from Nature and
Engraved in Aqua-Tinta with a Description of Each
Animal*, 4to, 1788. Plate 16, Angora Goat.
Weidenfeld and Nicolson Archives, photographed by
Angelo Hornak at Bernard Quaritch Ltd.

142 Mark Catesby: *The Natural History of Carolina,
Florida and the Bahama Islands . . .* , 2 vols, large folio,
1731–43. Plate 57, Green-Snake. Linnean Society
Library, photo Angelo Hornak.

143 Mark Catesby: *The Natural History of Carolina,
Florida and the Bahama Islands . . . .* Plate 58,
Wampum-Snake. Linnean Society Library, photo
Angelo Hornak.

144 Augustin Johann Roesel von Rosenhof: *Historia
Naturalis Ranarum Nostratium in qua Omnes Earum
Proprietates, Praesertim quae ad Generationem Ipsarum
Pertinent, Fusius Enarrantur*, fulio, Nuremberg, 1758.
Plate 9, Tree Frog. Linnean Society Library, photo
Angelo Hornak.

146 Augustin Johann Roesel von Rosenhof: *Historia
Naturalis Ranarum . . . .* Plate 8. British Museum
(Natural History).

148–9 Edward Donovan: *The Natural History of
British Fishes, Including Scientific and General Descriptions
of the Most Interesting Species, and an Extensive Selection
of Accurately Finished Coloured Plates. Taken Entirely
from the Original Drawings*, 5 vols, 8vo, 1802–6. Plate
10, Pike. British Museum (Natural History).

150–1 John Whitchurch Bennett: *A Selection from the
Most Remarkable and Interesting Fishes Found On the
Coast of Ceylon*, 4to, 1830. Plate 2. British Museum
(Natural History).

152–3 Etienne Geoffroy St Hilaire and Baron
Georges Leopold Chrétien Frédéric Dagobert de
Cuvier: *Histoire Naturelle des Mammifères*, 4 or 7 vols,
large folio, 1818–42. Male Leopard. Linnean Society
Library, photo Angelo Hornak.

155 Johann Christian Schreber: *Die Säugthiere in
Abbildungen nach der Natur mit Beschreibungen*, 4to,
Leipzig, 1804–10. Plate 307, *Galeopithecus variegatus
Geoffr*. British Museum (Natural History).

156–7 John James Audubon and John Bachman:
The Viviparous Quadrupeds of North America, 3 vols,
folio, New York, 1845–8. Plate 73, *Ovis Montana*.
British Museum (Natural History).

158 John Edwards Holbrook: *North American
Herpetology; or a Description of the Reptiles Inhabiting the
United States*, 5 vols, 4to, Philadelphia, 1842 (1st
edition 1836–40). Plate 13, *Emys insculpta*.

Weidenfeld and Nicolson Archives, photographed by
Angelo Hornak at Bernard Quaritch Ltd.

160–1 John James Audubon and John Bachman:
The Quadrupeds of North America, 3 vols, large 8vo,
New York, 1849–54. Black-Footed Ferret. Victoria
and Albert Museum (Cooper-Bridgeman Library).

162 John James Audubon: *The Birds of America from
Original Drawings Made During a Residence of Twenty
Five Years in the United States*, 4 vols, elephant folio,
1827–38. Plate 66, Barred Owl with a Grey Squirrel.
British Museum (Natural History).

163 John Cassin: *Mammalogy and Ornithology*. *United
States Exploration Expedition under Charles Wilkes*, folio,
Philadelphia, 1858. Plate 10, *Cervus macrotis*.
Weidenfeld and Nicolson Archives, photographed by
Angelo Hornak at Bernard Quaritch Ltd.

164–5 John Edward Gray: *Gleanings from the
Menagerie and Aviary at Knowsley Hall*, large folio,
Knowsley, 1846–50. Plate 6, Ielerang or Javan
Squirrel. Weidenfeld and Nicolson Archives,
photographed by Angelo Hornak at Bernard
Quaritch Ltd.

166–7 John Edward Gray: *Gleanings from the
Menagerie and Aviary at Knowsley Hall*. Plate 51,
Llamas. Linnean Society Library, photo Angelo
Hornak.

169 John Edward Gray: *Gleanings from the Menagerie
and Aviary at Knowsley Hall*. Plate 1, Vitoe. Linnean
Society Library, photo Angelo Hornak.

170–1 David Low: *The Breeds of the Domestic Animals
of the British Islands*, 2 vols, folio, 1842. Chillingham
Bull. Weidenfeld and Nicolson Archives,
photographed by Angelo Hornak at Bernard
Quaritch Ltd.

172 John James Audubon and John Bachman: *The
Quadrupeds of North America*, 3 vols, large 8vo, New
York, 1849–54. Plate 41, Polar Bear. Victoria and
Albert Museum (Cooper-Bridgeman Library).

174–5 William Houghton: *British Freshwater Fishes*,
folio, 1879. Grayling. British Museum (Natural
History).

176 Robert Fitzroy: *The Zoology of the Voyage of HMS
Beagle, Under the Command of Capt. Fitzroy During the
Years 1832–36. Ed. and Superintended by Charles Darwin*,
4to, 1838–43. Plate 27, *Reithrodon Chinchilloides*.
British Museum (Natural History).

181 Augustin Johann Roesel von Rosenhof:
Insectenbelustigung, 4to, Nuremberg, 1740–c. 1759.
Title page to Part II. Linnean Society Library, photo
Angelo Hornak.

182 J. J. Ernst: *Insectes d'Europe, Peints d'après Nature*,
8 vols, large 4to, Paris, 1779–93. Title page.
Weidenfeld and Nicolson Archives, photographed by
Angelo Hornak at Bernard Quaritch Ltd.

183 Moses Harris: *The Aurelian: Or, Natural History of
English Insects; namely Moths and Butterflies. Together
with the Plants on Which They Feed; a Faithful Account of
Their Respective Changes; Their Usual Haunts when in the
Winged State; and Their Standard Names, as Given and
Established by the Worthy and Ingenious Society of
Aurelians. Drawn, Engraved and Coloured from the
Natural Subjects Themselves*, folio, 1758–66. Plate 36.
British Museum (Natural History).

184 Dru Drury: *Illustrations of Natural History;
Wherein Are Exhibited Upwards of 240 Figures of Exotic
Insects, According to Their Different Genera, Very Few of
Which Have Hitherto Been Figured by Any Author*, 3 vols,
4to, 1770–82. Vol. I, Plate 49. Linnean Society
Library, photo Angelo Hornak.

185 Edward Donovan: *An Epitome of the Natural
History of the Insects of India and the Islands in the Indian
Sea*, 4to, 1800–4. Plate 21, *Papilio Ulysses*. Linnean
Society Library, photo Angelo Hornak.

186 Benjamin Wilkes: *Twelve New Designs of British
Butterflies*, folio, 1742. Plate 1. Weidenfeld and
Nicolson Archives, photographed by Angelo Hornak
at Bernard Quaritch Ltd.

187 Franz Michael Regenfuss: *Auserlesne Schnecken,
Muscheln und Andere Schaalthiere auf Allerhöchsten Befehl
Sr Konigl. Majest. nach den Originalen Gemalt, in Kupfer
Gestochen, und mit Natürlichen Farben Erleuchtet*, 2 vols,
large folio, Copenhagen, 1758. Plate 2. British
Museum (Natural History).

188 Georg Wolfgang Knorr: *Les Délices des Yeux et de
l'Esprit, ou Collection Générale des Différentes Espèces de
Coquillages que la Mer Renferme*, 6 vols, 4to,
Nuremberg, 1760–73. Title page to Part II.
Weidenfeld and Nicolson Archives, photographed by
Angelo Hornak at Bernard Quaritch Ltd.

190 Thomas Martyn: *The Universal Conchologist,
Exhibiting the Figure of Every Known Shell Accurately
Drawn and Painted After Nature*, 4 vols, folio, 1784–7.
Plate 30. British Museum (Natural History).

191 George Perry: *Conchology, or the Natural History of
Shells: Containing a New Arrangement of the Genera and
Species, Illustrated by Coloured Engravings Executed from
the Natural Specimens and Incl. The Latest Discoveries*,
folio, 1811. *Pyrula*. Weidenfeld and Nicolson
Archives, photographed by Angelo Hornak at
Bernard Quaritch Ltd.

Index